2 LIVE 4

WHY DID YOU THINK YOU WERE HERE?

RYAN DOBSON

WITH
MARCUS BROTHERTON

Multnomah® Publishers *Sisters, Oregon*

2 LIVE 4
published by Multnomah Publishers, Inc.

© 2005 by James Dobson, Inc.
International Standard Book Number: 1-59052-474-8

Cover photo by Stephen Gardner, PixelWorksStudio.net

Scripture quotations are from:
The Holy Bible, New International Version
© 1973, 1984 by International Bible Society,
used by permission of Zondervan Publishing House
Other Scripture quotations are from:
The Message
© 1993, 1994, 1995, 1996, 2000, 2001, 2002
Used by permission of NavPress Publishing Group

Multnomah is a trademark of Multnomah Publishers, Inc.,
and is registered in the U.S. Patent and Trademark Office.
The colophon is a trademark of Multnomah Publishers, Inc.

Printed in the United States of America

For information:
MULTNOMAH PUBLISHERS, INC.
601 N. LARCH ST.
SISTERS, OREGON 97759

Library of Congress Cataloging-in-Publication Data
Dobson, Ryan.
  2 live 4 / Ryan Dobson with Marcus Brotherton.
     p. cm.
ISBN 1-59052-474-8
  1. Christian life. I. Title: To live for. II. Brotherton, Marcus. III.
Title.
  BV4501.3.D62 2005
  248.4—dc22

                                              2005025589

05 06 07 08 09 10—10 9 8 7 6 5 4 3 2 1 0

*This book is dedicated to the woman I'm on a lifelong
journey with, my wife, Laura.
For better or for worse, in good times and bad,
in sickness and health I'll be with you.
What a journey it will be!*

CONTENTS

Special Thanks

I have more people to thank than pages or words. First and foremost I thank my amazing group of friends from whom I get my inspiration and encouragement. To those I've known a lifetime and those only a short while, I love you all. I also couldn't have finished this book without the incredible help from my friends at Multnomah. To Don for first believing in me, and to Jason for all the support and belief in this message. Lastly but surely not least to Thomas and Marcus for helping me put my ideas and words onto the pages of this book. For the edits, rewrites, late nights, and brain storms, I'm proud of this book and I'm honored to have worked with you.

God bless you all,
Ryan

ɬ

When You Ride to Hell's Kitchen

Whenever I ride to Hell's Kitchen, my chest always tightens. You just never know what can happen at a place like this.

Hell's Kitchen is a burger joint on a twisted road between Riverside County and Orange County. Outside there's always about a hundred Harleys. Inside, riders sport tattoos and beer guts. Black leather jackets are everywhere. Hell's Kitchen's got a condiment bar built out of a casket. **When you lift a stick shift with a skull on it, the lid rises** and you can load up on ketchup, mustard, and onions. You can smell the gasoline and French fries from a mile away.

If you want a hamburger the easy way, you can always go to McDonald's.

In some motorcycle circles, there's a definite chain of command. Custom Harleys are the biggest, baddest kids on the street. They aren't particularly nimble and they're not known for mechanical reliability. But Harleys wear the badge of more than a hundred years of American grit. They've roared down every open road. They have been in movies. They have been to war. Heck, Evil Knievel even jumped a Harley! They symbolize liberty, fortitude, attitude—everything that's resolute about a person's soul. If you show up at Hell's Kitchen, you need all that. Fact is, if you're riding anything except a Harley Davidson, you may not finish all your burger. You may not even get through the front door.

I don't ride a Harley.

Whenever I pull up outside Hell's Kitchen, **the questions begin.**

"Whaddya got there?" a biker will grunt and take a few steps toward me.

"Never seen one of those," another will say. He's not making an observation. He's accusing me of something, and it's not good.

Things seem to cool when the bikers start looking over my bike a little closer. It's a thirty-year-old Triumph, a British bike, styled like a café racer. I bought it about four years ago for three-thousand dollars from a guy who owns a tattoo shop. I bet I've put four thousand into it since then. There are no gauges, no speedometer. It used to be silver with flames and iron crosses. Now it's just flat black.

Usually when the crowd at Hell's Kitchen sees my bike up close, there's a sense of admiration. I'm not just some kook, they soon realize, and I'm just here for the food like the rest of them. After the crowd around my bike has lessened, the remaining bikers nod with a gesture that means I'm welcome past the front door.

Mostly the Hell's Kitchen crowd wants to make sure I'm not a "trailer queen"—it's not exactly the politest term, but then again, this is not exactly the politest crowd. Trailer queens are considered the frauds of the motorcycle world. They're phonies, hypocrites—people who load their bikes onto trailers and take them to shows. Trailer queens don't want to feel the wind and sun of the unprotected road for any distance, or risk getting grease and grime on their well-pressed Dockers. A trailer queen would rather sit in the air-conditioned comfort of a minivan than ride into the teeth of a hard wind.

As I ease into the plastic seats of the restaurant, I remind myself that eating one of the best burgers in California isn't always the easiest thing to do. But then again, if eating at Hell's Kitchen were easy, every trailer queen would do it.

WHEN YOU WANT SOMETHING MORE

You can't just own a bike and leave it at that—not if you call yourself a rider. You have to ride. You have to take it out of your garage with your sunglasses on, crank the starter, open the throttle, and take off down the road. In the same way, there are some people who call themselves

Christians who are really trailer queens at heart. It's easy to sit in church and call ourselves Christians. Anyone can do that.

It's easy to think of salvation as a free ticket to heaven.

Problem solved. Case closed.

But Christianity is more than an insurance policy against hell. Just because you're not going to hell tomorrow doesn't mean you're really living today. Any beer gut at Hell's Kitchen can tell you that.

Even if we wouldn't actually categorize ourselves as trailer-queen Christians, there are a lot of us who are up against a wall when it comes to the Christian faith. It feels like we're stuck. We've been to church, but **something isn't clicking** for us. For some reason, we don't have the transformed life that preachers always talk about. We don't have a life we'd highly recommend to anyone.

There's got to be more than this, we think. Even if we don't say it.

I was speaking at a broadcaster's convention back east when a man walked up to me and handed me a card.

"Isn't this great?" he asked. I could see he was really excited about it.

It was a small yellow card that said: "Get Out of Hell Free" on one side and a brief formula for getting to heaven on the other.

I didn't know what to say. I'm not questioning the guy's sincerity. But something rubbed me wrong about this tract.

"Um, yeah, it's really…yellow," was all I could think to say.

It was kind of a stupid answer, I realize now. I hope the guy wasn't offended. But in light of where I've been the past couple of years, it was just hard to view something that seemed to box up the Christian message as tidy as that tract did. Jesus Christ offers something so amazing, so mysterious, so incomprehensibly more than we could dare ask or imagine—a "Get Out of Hell Free" card just seemed so inconsequential. Like Jesus is the card you needed to win at Monopoly.

Is that all He is?

Do you know that story in Matthew 14 where Peter walks on water? This is Peter we're talking about here—a rough and tumble fisherman, a guy who knows boats, a guy who can pull nets and pick fish all night.

Peter looks up to see Jesus standing on the waves with the wind all around Him. Jesus says: "Take courage. It's me. Don't be afraid."

"Lord, if it's you," Peter replies, "tell me to come to you on the water."

"Come on over," Jesus says.

So there's Peter, getting out of the boat, taking steps on a sea he's been trying not to drown in all his life. Peter knows that liquid can't hold him up! But he's walking anyway.

Anytime I've heard that story growing up in Sunday school or church, it was always about how Peter blew it because he didn't keep his eyes on Christ and sank instead. But have you ever thought we might be missing the obvious point? *Peter was walking on water here!* Peter! Standing on water! Can you see how crazy that is?

I've been around water as long as I can remember. I'm a surfer. I know the properties of water. It's impossible to walk on it. But Peter's like, "Lord, if You tell me I can do it, I can do it."

That's what our relationship with Jesus can be like.

A connection with Christ in our lives right now is a bond with the God of the Universe.

He's greater than anything we can think of. And He didn't just give us life so maybe—if we believe the right four things—we won't go to hell when we die.

King David wrote "Better is one day in your courts than a thousand elsewhere" (Psalm 84:10). Here's what that simple statement tells me: Out of all the incredible things David had seen and experienced in the world, what he wanted most was to experience life in the presence of God.

That's what I want to talk about in this book. **What would cause David to be so captivated with God?** God is the same as He's always been, and whatever David had is that same something that's available to us today. It's not that heaven doesn't matter. Or believing the right things. Or getting saved. It's just that heaven is not the whole prize. Jesus Christ offers a way of living right now that's better than we could ever imagine. In John 10, Jesus offered His followers *abundant* life. He didn't say magic life. Or perfect. Or painless. He said abundant. Abundant means a life that is so full of real living that you can't stop it. It overflows like a fountain, maybe even on bad days. It splashes others with life too. That's abundant.

Is that something you crave? Or are you satisfied to sit in the minivan? Maybe hand out a few tracts.

I don't know if *abundant* is a word we use too much today, but listen—it definitely tells me that **Jesus promises us a lot more than just a life that isn't miserable.** Much more than your average, run of the mill, stuck in a rut, going nowhere, bored out of your mind, no purpose, no direction, no vision, no passion life.

COME, MEET A WILDMAN

In the pages ahead, I want to show you what it means to press forward into the teeth of life with purpose, courage, and adventure. Think of this book as an invitation to meet a Person truly worth living for. A relationship with Jesus Christ is not about being dull and boring and just hanging on until we get to heaven. It's an amazing journey to be on right now, however old you are, wherever you're at in life.

It's hard to just give you words here. Words don't do justice to a relationship with Jesus Christ. I think that's why Christ Himself used stories when He talked about His connection to God. Jesus would point out whatever was around Him, and compare what He was talking about to what people could see, touch, and experience. "Check out that light on a hill over there," He'd say to His disciples. "I want you to be like that—something intense and clear that everybody can see."

So mostly in this book, I'll be telling you stories about how Christ is real to me and can be real to you—in this world now. Your relationship with Christ is bound to look different than mine. This isn't a paint-by-numbers book where I hand you answers and you know three things to do afterwards. **I'm not about giving answers,** I'm about introducing you to Someone who shows you how to live.

I recognize, too, that I live in a sub-culture that few people experience. I live in a suburb of Los Angeles, about two miles from the Pacific Ocean. I surf and ride a skateboard, I jump out of airplanes and ride my motorcycle too fast, and I talk to people all over the country about Jesus Christ. That's what I do for a living. It's not that my life is better than anyone else's. But I recognize I live very differ-

ently from a student in Boston or a programmer in
Chicago or a sixty-five-year-old farmer in Nebraska. How
Jesus guides my life will not look the same as how He
guides yours. In this book, I'm not encouraging you to live
like I do. I'm encouraging you to live for one Person only,
that's Jesus Christ. He's the true Wildman.

When you mention the term "abundant life," **a lot
of Christians start to think about the
boatload of cash** that God will surely give them, or
the autograph-giving celebrity they're going to become for
God. But having an abundant life has nothing to do with
possessions or fame, it's about what we're doing with truth.
It's about heart and actions—it's who we are and what we
do. The writer of Galatians describes it as fruit—spiritual
fruit—stuff we grow that yields a payoff that will last forever.

Sometimes when we live the abundant life, the Lord
will take us on a path that looks anything but abundant.
Christ never promises that we won't experience hard times;
His promise is that He'll be with us through them.

Take it from me. I've been there.

IN THE SWEAT OF LIFE

Six years ago I was living the American dream. At age 29, I
had everything a young man could want. I was working as
a computer technician, making pretty good money. I vol-
unteered in a large church. Using some early inheritance

money from my family, my wife and I bought a house near the lake and golf course in Mission Viejo, an affluent area of southern California. It was an absolutely great house—not huge by area standards—but it had high ceilings and walk-in closets, and we filled it with furniture, a pool table, a pinball machine, and a big TV.

From the outside, my life looked perfect. Inside, I was a mess.

It's always tricky to talk about problems in a marriage. Right now, you're only hearing from me—and there are two sides to everything. But let's just say my wife and I weren't getting along very well. I'm five-foot-ten and today I weigh about 175 pounds. Back then I weighed 135. It wasn't because I was healthy. It was because I was too stressed to eat. I was having nightmares and panic attacks. I was taking a variety of medications for depression and anxiety. The truth of my life was a dark cloud. One day on the way home from church my wife said to me: "This isn't what I signed up for." That was the beginning of the end.

Divorce is horrible. There is no other way to describe it. Maybe you know firsthand, too. I had made mistakes in my marriage, but I didn't want it to end. I fought for it as long as I could, then it all collapsed.

The very same day, I phoned my father about 10 p.m. I remember our conversation word-for-word.

"Hey, how's it going?" he said.

"Not good," I replied.

"What do you mean?" he asked.

"I need to come home," I said. And then I started crying.

I've always been pretty good friends with my parents, Jim and Shirley Dobson. Home to me is southern California, but right then, home felt like where they were, in Colorado. I needed to go home. I needed my family.

But **my dad surprised me** with the next thing he said. "Can I call you right back?"

This is every child's fear—your father is too busy to help when you need him most. Here I was, the lowest I've ever been, and my dad cut short our conversation. As head of Focus on the Family, my dad has devoted his life to strengthening marriages and families. I knew that having his son get divorced would break my parents' hearts. But with dad in the national spotlight, I knew my failures could hurt their ministry too, maybe even damage the organization. This was just the sort of thing the tabloids love to pick up on.

Staring at the phone, I thought, "Maybe I've messed up too much. Maybe my dad finally thinks I'm a complete idiot."

One minute later the phone rang. It was my dad again.

"Okay, I've just got you booked for an 8 a.m. flight tomorrow to Colorado," he said. "Will that be early enough for you?"

I breathed a sigh of relief.

Then we both cried.

A divorce doesn't happen all at once. It can take months, sometimes years for everything to unravel completely. And it usually takes years to get hearts and lives stitched back together again, too.

To set the record straight: my divorce was not because of adultery, an emotional affair or abuse. I'm not trying to justify it here, and I can't quite explain all the reasons for it. But it happened. It was very real. And it hurt like hell. If you're like most people these days, you can probably point to something in your life, or in the lives of those you dearly love, that ranks right up there for pain and loss and failure.

Two years later I found myself living alone in a tiny apartment, spitting distance from ten lanes of freeway. My job was gone. The house was gone. I didn't volunteer at the church anymore. Bills piled up around me until I was overwhelmingly in debt. I seldom went out. My life consisted of watching TV and eating fast food. Often I slept sixteen hours a day.

"Lord," I prayed, "You promised an abundant life. But I've never been more miserable. Are You still with me? Do You still care?"

Do you know that passage in 1 Kings 19 where God
speaks to the prophet Elijah in a whisper? The Lord leads
Elijah to a cave where a powerful windstorm occurs, but
God is not in the wind. Then there's an earthquake, but
God's not there either. After the earthquake comes a fire,
but still no God. After the fire comes a gentle whisper.
When Elijah hears this, he pulls his cloak about him, stands
at the mouth of the cave, and prepares to listen to what
God has to say.

My whisper from God came in the form of a phone
call from my friend, Dave.

"You may not want to hear this just yet," Dave said.
"But I promise you, it'll get better."

Dave was right. I still had hope. As strange as it
sounded, I knew God was good, even though I was walking
through the darkest valley of my life. I knew that God
loved me, was there for me, and was going to take care of
me in the midst of whatever mess I was in. But I didn't
understand Jesus' words that He would give me abundant
life.

Honestly, I doubt if the abundant life is anything that
can be taught in a seminar. You just can't fully describe it.
You just have to live it. For me, I had to lose everything
before I could begin to understand what it meant. Only
when I had absolutely nothing was I ready to hear God say:
"You've tried it your way. Now try it Mine."

I love how Eugene Peterson paraphrases the words of
Jesus in Matthew 11 in *The Message*: "Are you tired? Worn

out? Burned out on religion?" Jesus says. "Come to me and you'll recover your life. Walk with me and work with me. Learn the unforced rhythms of grace. Keep company with me, and you'll learn to live freely and lightly."

That was where I was at, and I was willing.

LIKE THE SUN ON CATALINA

About six months ago, I woke up in a new apartment in San Clemente. This one's a bit bigger, and it's not near a freeway. It's near an elementary school, in fact, and a park, and when you look out the window, down a valley, you can see the ocean about two miles away.

Moving here was tough. It had been raining for days, and it poured the night I moved my stuff. If you think it never rains in southern California, believe me it does. It just tends to fall all at once. My cardboard boxes dissolved. Everything got muddy and damp. It was a tough transition after a tough couple of years.

But the morning after I moved dawned clear and calm. I opened the window. Outside, the air had that just-washed smell. Streets looked rinsed and fresh. Everything appeared new. I stood there in pajama bottoms, taking it all in.

And then I heard it:

OH BEAUTIFUL, FOR SPACIOUS SKIES, FOR AMBER WAVES OF GRAIN...

Classes were beginning in the school across the street, and all the kids had come outside to sing patriotic songs at the start of their day. There they all stood, voices bright, faces upturned. Some of the littler ones held hands. From my window I could look down and see the Pacific. The sun was hitting Catalina Island with just the right angle to make it shine.

You know, I received that morning as the Lord's word to me, His word not in a voice but in a living picture—an image of music and vibrancy and color and clarity that I'll never forget. "I'm with you," God said. "And the life you have with me is always rich."

Are you with me? That's the life I want us to talk about together in this book. Just on a practical, day-to-day basis what would that kind of life look like, and what's keeping so many from experiencing it?

It's true, only Christ can save you from hell. But only Christ can give you life to the full now, too.

Only He can help you know it and believe in it and grab hold of it.

The abundant life.

It's the life you were meant 2 Live 4.

2

The Stretch
of Faith

I like how Genesis talks about God walking in the Garden of Eden in the cool of the day. There's Adam—all his work done, everything peaceful, everything quiet, and God comes by just to catch up.

I often picture God that way as I'm paddling out on my surfboard on a cool morning. The hot sun won't be up yet. Fog lies low along the coastline. The farther out you get, you can't see the shore anymore. The only way you know your direction is by the flow of the sea. Sometimes it's so cold you can see your breath. You get so focused; all you can hear is the rubbery sound of your wetsuit as you paddle east with the waves against your board.

Far out in the ocean, I'll stop and wait for the right wave. It's then I get the fullest sense of the presence of the Lord. *The same God who created all this is here, right now,* I think to myself. The same

Being who designed dolphins and whales, tides and the pull of the planets is out there on the water with me. The same God who walked in Eden in the evenings loves me and knows me by name. If I listen, He has things to say.

Living abundantly comes in so many ways. At its core it is a knowledge that God is always with us, and that He is always good. It's more than knowledge, actually—it's a confidence, an assurance. No matter what we go through, no matter where we end up, we trust that God is there, and that He always has our best interest in mind.

Strangely, as God shows us what it means to live an abundant life, He often takes us to a place where it feels like He's disappeared. Perhaps we're up against an obstacle that seems like it can't be overcome. Maybe we've been struck with a blow that lays us flat. Maybe we've come to a place where we have no idea which way to turn.

The temptation at those times is to quit whatever quest we're on. We forget that the presence of the Lord is always with us. **We forget that He's everywhere—** He's with us when we surf and when we drive our cars and eat lunch and watch movies and go out on dates and go to work and come home again.

There's that verse in 2 Corinthians 12:9 where Paul has prayed three times for God to take away some sort of affliction. We don't know what hardship it was, but God's only reply is that **His grace is sufficient,** and His power is made perfect in weakness.

That's a strange idea— when we are weak, God is strong.

Could it be true? When life gets hard, God is there. It's easy to get tired, frustrated, or discouraged—we think there will be no way to continue going in the direction we're called to go.

But at times like those, the Lord says, "This is still the life you were meant to live. But now you need faith."

UP AGAINST THE WALL

A friend of mine named Joe White showed me this. Joe is president of Kanukuk Kamps, a fantastic network of sports camps located across Missouri and Colorado. When I was in the middle of the hardest season of my life, Joe phoned me up and asked me how it was going.

I know he knew the answer. I couldn't even say anything.

"Come to camp," Joe said. He didn't say much more than that, but I knew what he meant. It was an offer—an invitation for me to click off the TV, get outside, and keep moving forward.

I turned him down. I was losing my house. I had court dates to keep. I needed to go look for a new job. Besides, I was thirty years old by then. I didn't think camp was the answer to my problems.

But Joe phoned again. And again, and again.

"Fine," I said at last, disgusted with myself more than anything. "I'll go."

It was a step for me, a stretch of faith. I didn't feel like doing anything except existing by that time. At my lowest, I could honestly say I didn't care about anything—not myself, or God, or life. All I wanted to do was sit and eat fast food and watch the world go by from the safety of my couch.

Going to camp turned out to be the greatest thing I could have done. I got up at a regular hour. I ate real food. I went down to the dock each day and swam. I started reading my Bible more. Jesus and I had some of the realest conversations we've ever had. Have you ever told Him exactly how you feel? Have you ever told the Lord that your life feels like garbage?

Have you ever opened a vein to God and left nothing hidden?

He is able to handle all that. It's funny—we can talk with our friends about what's truly happening in our lives, but when we approach Jesus we feel we need to clean up our act first. When we try to pray we feel we need to praise Him first, or maybe confess our sins or sing a hymn or something. We convince ourselves we don't feel like doing any of those things, so we end up not talking to Him at all.

But the Lord is capable of so much more than we give Him credit for. He can handle all we throw at Him. Hebrews 4:15 describes Jesus Christ as Someone who is able to sympathize with *all* our weaknesses. Everything we've ever done or been through or thought or said. He can relate. I believe it's a reverent thing to trust the Lord with how we truly feel.

My life didn't change instantly after I came back from camp. But what stuck with me most was that I kept going. I didn't stay in my apartment and die.

I didn't keep going on my own strength. I kept going on faith. When God asks us to live by faith, He asks that we come to Him despite our failures. God knows our limitations and our weaknesses. When we approach Him by faith we approach Him not knowing what the outcome of our lives will be. Our only belief is that He is good, and that whatever we go through, He is with us.

Faith is confidence that God is who He says He is,

PERIOD.

THE STEEPER IT GETS, THE STEEPER IT BECOMES

Have you noticed that when you finish one challenge in your life, instead of a time of rest, there's often another challenge right after it—only this one is more difficult than the one before?

Once I was backpacking just north of Yosemite National Park. I was one of the leaders on this trip with a bunch of kids. Ten days. Forty miles. Each of us carrying a seventy-pound backpack. We hiked over high cliffs and around steep waterfalls, through meadows and between giant Sequoias. The scenery was incredible, but the trip as a whole was just plain hard. Sometimes one of the kids wouldn't be able to carry all his stuff, so we as leaders would need to pick up the slack. It got cold at night. I don't know who was in charge of food for that trip, but everything we ate tasted like clay. To top it all off, when the trip ended, we still had one requirement left to go. **At eight-thousand feet we all dropped our packs and went for a five mile run.**

Who was the lightbulb that thought up that one?

But there was actually something cool about that last part of the trip. We were all exhausted—we thought we were finished. We had convinced ourselves that we were at the end of our ropes, and the only safe solution now was to sit, rest, and go home.

Then—surprise—along comes the run.

You learn something about yourself at a time like that. You're able to tap into strength you didn't know existed. You stretch yourself beyond what you know is secure. And then you're doing it—right in the middle of something you never thought was possible—and then it's finished, and you've got a great story to tell to your grandkids some day.

That's part of what goes into an amazing life. When we are pushed to places where we've never been before—places we feel we can't go on our own strength—we grow in ways we never would on our own. Living by faith takes us beyond our own resources. Our peak is reached. Our strength is gone. We come to a place where we can't survive without Jesus, and we find that's not a bad place to be. Why? Because once we're there, He is able to do things we could never do on our own.

And our faith in action is what allows that kind of life to happen.

When the prophet Jeremiah raised the faith issue with God, He replied in the form of a question: "If you have raced with men on foot and they have worn you out, how can you compete with horses?" He asked. "If you stumble in safe country, how will you manage in the thickets by the Jordan?" (Jeremiah 12:5). In other words, if Jeremiah couldn't trust God in a time of peace and safety, how could he ever manage when the going got tough?

Jeremiah needed to stretch his faith if he was ever going to be in the place God wanted him to be.

Do you want an amazing life? If your answer is yes, what are you looking for in your character, relationships, accomplishments, and work? **The way you get there is by going places you didn't think you could go.** God wants to take you places where you can't do things unless you rely on Him. Why? Because when you're stripped down to just faith and not much else, that's when Jesus can be the Lord of your life. And that's when the abundant life really kicks in.

Author and church leader Ray Stedman describes the abundant life this way: "It's filled with constant expectation of what is coming next. Sometimes it's dangerous, sometimes it hurts, but it's always filled with a sense of adventure."

OVER THE HANDLEBARS

I have a good friend who met this girl. She had it all—eyes, hair, smile—enough to keep a bunch of poets busy for weeks. One of the best things about her was that she liked mountain biking. This was a girl worth investing some serious time in, said my friend.

So off they went on a date. No dinner and a movie. No picnic in the park. No evening at the opera. They loaded their bikes on the top of his truck and headed for the mountains.

I don't know if you've ever been hardcore mountain biking before. I think the best part is flying downhill.

Leaves and branches whiz past. Sometimes the trails get so narrow you're brushing trees with both elbows. Stumps and boulders jump up in your path. Creeks and mud show up without warning. You have to be comfortable with a certain amount of reckless abandon to make it on a mountain bike.

So there's my buddy and his new female friend, flying down this steep hill having a great time—until she hits the front brakes too hard and goes over the handlebars.

Have you ever seen a rag doll get tossed by a child across a room? This girl flew about ten feet and crashed face down into the dirt. All around her were rocks and sticks. This was definitely no soft landing.

My friend heard the accident and freaked out. He was just getting to know this girl, and already she had broken something, he was sure. She'd probably need surgery. She had probably ripped her whole face off.

He rushed up to help, but he was in for a shock. The girl stood up, straightened her handlebars, spit dirt out of her mouth, and laughed. Then she said, "We've got to do that again!"

At that moment, my friend knew this was the girl for him. And sure enough, they got married.

That story teaches me about faith. **Faith is an unshakable assurance—not that life will be comfortable, but that life will be hard AND good.** Life is kind of like biking up a hill and flying down again. Life is hitting the brakes too hard and getting tossed over the handlebars. Faith? Faith is brushing yourself off and getting back on. It's the wild ride with the One you're getting to know. It's the moment of knowledge that the One you're with is the One you love.

The funny thing about my friend and his new wife is that their adventures haven't stopped. Just before they got married they had one of those serious conversations where everything got laid on the line. He told her that he definitely didn't want to have kids because he had this dream of being an author and he thought writing would take so much of his time and energy that there wouldn't be any left over for kids. She, however, definitely wanted kids. So this was the deal-breaker for them both.

They agreed to pray about it and let God change their hearts. **Of course, my friend told me later he was positive God would see things his way** and change her heart. But that's not what happened. Today they have a whole herd of kids. She's a great mother, and he's a great dad as well as a great husband. Oh, and a skilled author too.

That's what faith can do for you.

In Psalm 139: 23–24 David talks about how God knows him in every way, and how he has abandoned himself to God's plan for his life—"Search me, O God," David writes, "and know my heart; test me and know my anxious thoughts. See if there is any offensive way in me, and lead me in the way everlasting."

Faith lets God refine, revise, even reverse our plans and

dreams. Faith says: "My life is in Your hands, God, and You are good. What amazing things do You have for my life today?"

TO A PLACE WE'VE NEVER BEEN

Think of faith as your choice to release the emergency brake of your life so Christ can put you in motion, into a purposeful progress toward the abundant life He wants for you. Forward motion usually requires a willingness to grow, to stretch past what's easy or familiar.

The other day I was out surfing with my twin nephews. They're eleven. These kids are maybe a foot shorter than me, but already they can ride the waves like Moondoggy and the Great Kahuna.

Waves were absolutely pounding that day—the type of surf that makes you think maybe you should take up golf. But we paddled out anyway into some of the biggest breakers I had ever seen. It was awesome. **Scary. Amazing.** Water like that shoves you around and rolls over you, but when you finally catch your wave it's like dropping into the deepest, fastest, most beautiful swimming pool you've ever seen.

That day, my nephews and I definitely had to push ourselves. We were surfing way past our capacity in those waves. I did okay. But my nephews did great. They are going to be incredible surfers someday.

Faith is like that. It involves stretching. Sometimes we need to paddle out to the big waves, the ones that seem too big for us. Stretching increases our capacity to trust the Lord. When you trust Him, it's like you're not afraid of anything anymore. What used to seem impossible becomes possible.

I've noticed that Christ doesn't ever call us to some kind of plateau. We're not here to level off, to get stagnant or ho-hum, especially in our personal relationship with Him. The Christian life is more like a series of climbs, of peaks and valleys. Sometimes we find ourselves in a valley, or in a season of slowness or recharging. Sometimes we're on the peaks, absolutely amazed at how far we've come. Most of our life, though, is probably a slow climb.

Regardless of where you are, your invitation begins today. **Jesus is saying to you: "Come along, walk with me** in the cool of the day and I'll take you to places you've never been.

The journey won't always be easy, but it will always be good."

What He is asking right now is for you and me to release ourselves into His goodness and care. He calls that faith. Faith is not His best plan for taking us into the abundant life. It's the only plan. It's step one.

3

Loosening the Death Grip

The other day a friend who's been working at his job for a while complained to me about the low pay.

"Why don't you ask for a raise?" I asked.

"I will," he answered. "But before I ask for a raise I figure I've got to show up on time for work for at least six months first."

I asked him how often he was late.

"Oh, three, four days a week at least."

That's a problem. I love this guy but his work attitude shows why we're sometimes called the Entitlement Generation. Too many of us think we have a right to the good life, whether we've actually earned it or not.

Know anyone like that? Of course, slackers come in all age categories, and there are plenty of people running around with plugs and green hair who are just as focused, responsible, and hard-working as the suits in the board rooms.

Age doesn't matter, if you have an entitlement attitude, you have poison in your blood.

Sooner or later, it will pull you down. It will steal what life you have, not give you more for free.

When entitlement thinking sneaks into our faith, we lose. We might think God owes us His abundant life on our own terms. But it's not going to happen. We might think we've got a death grip on exactly what will bring us the most out of life.

But we're wrong.

Fact is, what we're hanging on to—our belief that life owes us, and owes us big—is the very thing that's keeping us from the truly amazing life God promises.

Let me show you what I mean.

WHEN WE FEEL LIKE IT'S OUR TURN

We slide into slacker spirituality when we feel God owes us something, or that we should be able to call all our own shots in life, or that the moral boundaries God sets are merely suggestions, or when we define God in our image.

An entitlement attitude says things like:

- I just don't know why I bother going to this worship service. I never get anything out of it.
- If God was really as good as everyone says He is, He wouldn't have let my Mom die as young as she did.
- There are a lot of other religions out there where things happen. I mean, there's power, and people tap into a strength that isn't theirs, and things really change. Nothing like that ever happens in Christianity.
- You and your girlfriend may have chosen to not have sex before marriage, but that's not what my girlfriend and I have decided. We just think that God's not as concerned about that as He used to be.
- I've been a Christian for a long time now, but how come other people live in bigger houses and drive better cars than I do? Is God unhappy with me? When am I going to get mine?

Entitlement says "I deserve this," and "These are my rights"—and that's all wrong.

Want a biblical portrait of entitlement? Look at the story Jesus told of the prodigal son and his family. You probably know the story in Luke 15. After the son wastes an inheritance on wild parties and prostitutes, he finally comes to his senses and runs home to his father's open arms. It's a story of the grace, forgiveness, and acceptance of a merciful God. And it's a good one.

But the story goes on to describe another person—the

older brother. He's a character we don't hear a lot about in sermons. While the family is celebrating the prodigal's safe return, the older brother is busy getting angry. "Look," he says to his father. "All these years I've been slaving for you and never disobeyed your orders. Yet you never gave me anything!"

Can you see the entitlement? "Where are my rights? What's coming to me here?" the older brother is saying. "I've been good! I deserve a reward!"

The father doesn't promise to make things better for the older brother. He just reminds him of what he already has but hasn't truly noticed. "My son," he says, "you are always with me, and everything I have is yours."

God reminds us of the same thing when He shows us how to live abundantly.

He doesn't promise us life will be a party in our honor. He's not out to check our wish lists and make sure we get each item on it. But like the father of the prodigal son, God has promised us *everything*. It's just that **most times, the everything we want is a lot different than the everything we need.** Only when we drop the slacker attitude and really set out to follow Jesus and do what He asks of us does abundant life *now* become a real possibility.

Of course, it's not always easy to take responsibility and follow the requirements. But if we don't, things can turn into a real mess. Can you imagine what would happen if we completely disregarded the owner's manual to our vehicles? I mean, I don't actually read the booklet that's crumpled in my glove compartment, but I *live by it.* When I pull up to a service station, I fill my truck with gasoline, not chocolate syrup. I've got to follow the manufacturer's specifications—I can't just do anything I feel like doing.

On a spiritual level, things operate the same way. When we fall for the lie that entitlement promises, we only do ourselves harm. We end up disappointed with other believers, wondering why our faith doesn't work as it should, and ultimately angry at God.

Genuine Christianity is about giving up our entitlement. It's putting down our pride and ego. It's shedding our claims to fame and fortune, comfort or satisfaction, or whatever we feel we absolutely have a right to and can't live without. **When we let go of our death grip on all our "rights and privileges," God can finally be God in our lives,** and we can finally get serious about following Him.

For example: I've got some surfer friends who had a great debate a while ago about ditching work to go surfing. As the story goes, one of their friends was on his way to his job and noticed some huge waves. It's not uncommon in the surfer community to pick up the cell phone at a time like that and twist the truth with a boss to rearrange priorities.

On this particular day, after the guy has made up some excuse to ditch work, he gets caught in some huge swells and almost doesn't make it back to shore. These surfers are all Christians, and some felt sympathetic toward the guy who almost lost his life. But others were saying that this was just a wake-up call. The whole "call in sick if the surf's up" mentality is really blowing it, they said, because it's a lie. As believers, we should stick to whatever we say we're going to do, they reasoned, even when there's good surf to be found.

These guys were wrestling with what it means to follow the truth. They were recognizing that a call to obedience is higher than a desire to do whatever they wanted to do. If they have a job, it just may be that the Lord would want them to go to it, even when the waves are good.

TAKE A RISK ON GOD

One of my best friends, Christopher, recently dislocated his leg at the knee. He got put in a cast from his toes to his hip. The guy has no insurance. His hours at work are limited because he can't stand up for very long anymore. But did he complain?

This is what he told me— word-for-word:

"I'm actually happy I hurt my leg. Now the Lord can show me the things He needs to."

No joke. Christopher was sincere. While he was in the hospital he got this strong sense that the Lord was telling him to use the experience of breaking his leg as an opportunity to pray. And not just pray by himself—to specifically pray out loud for people who needed it.

So there's my friend, working about three hours a day now—when anyone comes in he listens for the Lord to tell him if he or she needs prayer. When the Lord gives him the go ahead, he asks if he can pray for them. He's had people look shocked. People tell him all their troubles. He's had people cry, shake his hand, and give him hugs. All because he chose to be obedient to the Lord.

That's the abundant life.

Entitlement would say: *God, why did this happen to me? I don't deserve to hurt my leg.*

Trust says: *God, my life is in Your hands. What is Your plan to use this experience for Your glory?*

When Jesus Christ calls us to have a relationship with Him, He doesn't ask us to throw our brains out the window. But all our best-laid plans have limits, Christ says, and when we completely turn our lives over to Him, He is able to show us a life we never dreamed possible, a life without limits.

That's not always easy. It's hard not to fall into the trap of feeling entitled to something. **We watch all these stupid shows on TV that promote a consumer-oriented lifestyle.** It's easy to conclude that life is all about having more power or money or fame. Before long if we don't have these things, we get unhappy because we think we're not getting our fair share.

My friend Mike Yankoski just wrote a book called *Under the Overpass*. Mike made great grades at college. He planned to start a software company, which he'll probably still do someday—and I know he'll make great money at it. But during his sophomore year, he sensed the Lord was telling him to go be homeless for a while.

So he did.

For five months, in six different cities, he and a friend ate from dumpsters and slept under bridges. They were forced to depend on generosity and kindness. They witnessed firsthand more than five months of uncertainty, exhaustion, depression, and social rejection, all the time meeting the people who regularly live that life.

Why?

Sounds strange, but Mike wanted to. He knew that living abundantly requires risk. **He wanted to experience what it means to show God's love to some of the neediest people in the world.**

When we throw away our entitlement, it doesn't mean the Lord is going to ask us all to become homeless, or go be missionaries in Africa.

It's simply that the Lord asks us to take a risk on His Word, His goodness, His character, His record.

When we trust God like that, He works with us exactly where we are. He takes the rights and privileges we feel so impassioned about and transforms them into a different way of viewing the world. A sense of peace emerges. We don't have to figure out life—we don't have to scramble and claw our way to the top. God calls to us to be prepared, available, faithful, and dependable. When the time is right, God will move us where He wants us.

I've noticed that followers of Jesus who let go of their entitlement attitudes think, talk, and live differently. You'll hear them saying things like:

- Wow, Brandon and Trisha just bought a new house. My wife and I live in a shoebox, but instead of feeling jealous of them, we're happy that the Lord has chosen to give that to them. We pray they would use their new house for His glory.
- Here I am, 29 and single. I'd love to be married, but for some reason, the Lord has said no to that right now. God doesn't owe me anything in this area. He may never bring someone along. But He's still good, and I still trust Him.
- I just can't understand it. Everyone around me seems to be getting a great job. I went to the same college they did, but somehow I'm not where I want to be. Still, the Lord has me here for a reason. I can trust His timing in this season of life.

Giving up our entitlement allows us full rest. We don't have to be jealous of other people anymore, or angry that we didn't get ours (whatever "ours" is). God has brought them to a place for a reason different from ours. We can relax knowing that God has a plan for our lives, too—fuller and wilder than we could ever imagine. As we stay close to Him, He'll show us the right path.

ON A RIDE TO TRUSTING MORE

I learned a lot about entitlement on a long bike ride I took a couple years ago. It was right in the middle of my divorce, and a guy from Focus on the Family called and asked me if I wanted to participate in an event called "Bike Ride for the Family." The idea was to ride through all fifty states around America to raise funds for the ministry.

I can't say I was thrilled with the idea. I was feeling hurt and depressed. Why had my marriage failed when so many others have successful marriages? The last thing I felt like doing was helping out. When you're in a bad place, it's easy to feel entitled to your pain. You want to hold on to it tightly. "I've just been through the mud," you think, "so now I deserve to wallow."

Part of what I was feeling also came from this: it hasn't always been easy to grow up as I did, with my dad the founder and president of a national ministry. You get a little tired of being introduced as James Dobson's son. Or people will go: "Do you know my uncle—he works at Focus on the Family?" Well, no, there's like two thousand people who work there.

I also get the feeling that I'm not what they were expecting.

But on that trip a couple of things happened. We'd fly out to various places about twice a month and ride a three-day trip in each state. Each trip was about two hundred miles long. I ended up riding in twenty-three states overall. On each trip, maybe thirty or so people would start the ride together, but as the miles rolled on, the pack would string out, and I'd have a lot of time by myself to just ride and think.

This is what I thought about most: God's crazy plans.

When my dad started Focus back in the 1970s, he never set out to have a huge ministry. He had no idea what the organization was going to do. He only knew he was going to be obedient. His plan was to follow the Lord in whatever God had for him. He gave up whatever plans he had, and completely put his life in the hands of the Lord.

My mom was even more careful than my dad. I think she wanted him to go into private practice as a psychologist so they could have a quiet life together. She, too, could have played it safe and chosen not to follow the Lord's calling, but she didn't. She could have held back and never gotten involved in anything. But today she's head of the

National Day of Prayer movement. She and my dad regularly visit the White House, shaking hands with presidents.

As I pedaled along, I got to see firsthand the results of my parent's trust in God. I met so many people who told me they had been so touched by my parent's faithfulness to God's calling. In state after state, town after town, person after person I spoke to told me about how the Lord had helped them through Focus.

One guy was about seventy and came up to me with tears in his eyes. His marriage had fallen apart years ago, he said. He felt like he had lost everything and didn't know how he was going to continue. So he phoned up Focus on the Family. Focus arranged for private counseling for this guy for like six months, free of charge. They sent him all these books and tapes for free. The guy told me he would never have made it without this ministry.

On that trip I started feeling thankful for the upbringing I was privileged to have. I was impressed that the quiet faithfulness of two people, years ago, has resulted in seeing so many hearts and lives changed today. Entitlement is a temptation in any generation. If my parents had fallen into the trap of demanding what they wanted, they could have had a safer, less public life. But if they had done that, I doubt God would have ever used them in the way He has.

God has a reason and a plan for the paths He takes us on.

It doesn't matter if we're riding around the country on a bike, saying yes to beginning a national ministry, or turning off the TV, opening our Bibles, and saying "What do You want for my life, Lord?"

Christ's offer of the abundant life is waiting for us.

When we trade what we feel entitled to for what He promises, we begin to journey on the amazing path forward.

4

The Hardest Part

There are times when life just blasts ahead. We're cruising—wind in the hair, big silly grin on the face. Life is good. Everything is falling into place. *This is it!* we think. *This is the abundant life!*

Fantabulous!

And then there are other times when life stalls, or takes us into some kind of strange loop. The fun stops. Nothing seems to be happening. Nothing adds up. Everything is a big, fat waste. What we see when we look around isn't anything like what we expect or want. And it sure doesn't feel anything close to "abundant"!

What's a fully committed follower of Christ supposed to do then?

You might know the problem I'm talking about here. In fact, you might be in one of those strange loops right now in your life.

Then this chapter is for you.

WHEN GOD SLOWS THINGS DOWN

One of the toughest things about these wilderness seasons is that time seems to crawl. We're forced to just wait. Okay, God might be at work, but, wow, is He ever moving *s-l-o-w*!

And if you're like me, you hate to go slow.

Right after my divorce was a huge wilderness for me. I owned up to my part in bringing that season down on my own head, but still I wondered why my life took the course it did. I was completely depressed, hanging around all day watching TV. An abundant life? It sure didn't feel like it then.

If you've ever been in such a place, you know that **when we're forced to wait it's easy to throw hard questions at God.** *Does He really care about me? Has God forgotten about me? Is this really what the Christian life is all about?*

I know a guy named Pete who is this incredibly creative guy. He's got a production company and he makes these amazing videos that help show kids the way to Christ. Then Pete was diagnosed with colitis. If there was ever a crappy disease it's that. He had to have surgery on his colon. And then the incision got infected. And since then, the medication he took to clear up the infection has made his feet so numb he can hardly walk. For months all he's been able to do is sit around on his couch, trying to heal.

He's got a wife and three little kids. His disability insurance is set to run out soon. They're not sure how they're going to make it. One of the huge questions Pete is asking is: When am I ever going to get better?

Is this the journey God intends Pete to be on?

I've got another friend, Carrie, thirty-six and single. She's just an incredible girl—cute, funny, smart. She worked for a missions organization in her twenties, leading college kids on all these trips all over the world. After about ten years doing that she went back to graduate school to get her teaching degree. She spoke Spanish fluently by then and felt the Lord was calling her to work in the public school system, helping out the children of migrant workers. I know Carrie would love to be married someday, so why hasn't the Lord answered her prayer? She's serving Him wholeheartedly, why does He have her in this long, strange season of singleness?

Is Carrie living the abundant life Christ promises?

The problem with waiting is that it's easy to lose perspective. We can get worn down, tired of the battle, discouraged, or frustrated with where we're at. **At times like those we're tempted to find an easier way out.** The temptation is to conclude that the abundant life is found somewhere else. God's not delivering what we hoped He would, so it's our job to grab it anywhere we can.

That's one of the biggest mistakes we can make.

Abram blew it here. He stopped waiting for God's timing and launched out on his own, away from God's plan. In Genesis 12 through 17, we read how God told Abram (who was later known as Abraham) that his name would be great someday—he'd be the father of many nations, all people would be blessed through him.

But to do that Abram needed to have a son. Abram was fine with that—he longed for a son. In his culture, if you didn't have a son you were a disgrace. Abram began his spiritual journey by trusting God. He waited, prayed, and got busy with his wife, Sarai. But year after year went by, and still no son. So one day Sarai comes up with a plan. "Why don't you have a child with my servant, Hagar?" she says. "That way her child will be as good as ours."

Sounded good to Abram. So he has sex with Hagar, and she conceives a son, Ishmael. The Bible records a prophecy about Ishmael: "He will be a wild donkey of a man; his hand will be against everyone and everyone's hand against him, and he will live in hostility toward all his brothers" (Genesis 16:12).

A couple thousand years later, that prophecy is completely true. Ishmael is considered the father of the Arab people today. Nothing wrong with that, but the point is that Abram's decision not to wait for God's timing laid the groundwork for centuries of conflict to come.

Joseph is another guy God asks to wait. Joseph's track record is about the worst anyone could have. He starts out well enough—the favored son of Jacob, a wealthy herdsman living in Canaan. But when Joseph's brothers get jealous of him, they sell him as a slave to some Ishmaelite traders who take him down to Egypt. In Egypt, he quickly rises to the top level of Potiphar's house. But then Joseph gets framed for a crime he doesn't commit and ends up in prison.

Joseph's resume? Shepherd. Slave. Prisoner. Good luck landing a job with that kind of record! Is this what the abundant life is all about? The Bible says Joseph was seventeen years old when he went down to Egypt and thirty by the time he got out of prison. That's a long time waiting for something good to happen. But it does. In the course of one day, Joseph miraculously goes from prisoner to second-in-command over the whole country.

God knew what He was doing. God took His time in developing Joseph's character and skills for the amazing plans He had for his life. Joseph chose to trust God and wait for God's timing, even when the years were ticking away in an Egyptian jail.

Do you feel like you're in a holding pattern right now? When you look at your life, do you wonder why you're in the place you're in? Does it seem like the promises of God are far off, and you've been waiting and waiting for something better to appear that is nowhere in sight.

You may be exactly where the Lord wants you.

A SEASON FOR EVERYTHING

Sounds crazy, but waiting may be one of the best things God ever invented. It seems to be one of the most common tools He uses to shape us more like Christ. You see, even though it seems like we're going nowhere, some incredible things could be still happening in our life. While we wait, God can use that time to make us who we need to be. 2 Corinthians 3:18 talks about how we are continually being transformed into His likeness. **God uses every experience we go through to mold and shape us** to be more like Christ.

The writer of Ecclesiastes talks about how there is a season for everything—a time for every purpose under heaven. Life involves both ends of every spectrum. Sometimes we need to be quiet, sometimes we need to speak. Sometimes we need to mourn, sometimes we need to dance. Sometimes we're living all out—totally going places, doing things, meeting people, having the most amazing conversations—we feel like Jesus is as close as the air we breath. Then other times we're in seasons of discouragement or confusion. Life isn't as we hoped it would be. The only thing we know to do is to keep moving forward and be patient in the process.

That's all part of a rich, 2 Live 4 life. We need summer and winter. Pain and joy. Mountains and valleys. Ease and struggle. To be patient is huge. Some of these things God is doing in our lives can take years. If there's something we want that He isn't bringing our way, realize that He might be saying wait instead of no. Patience means we're not trying to arrive so fast. We take each day for what it is and appreciate it. Why should we rush life? Waiting doesn't hurt anything. Waiting means we're letting the Lord call us to something, instead of grabbing what we can.

It's God's plan then, not ours. He's in charge, not us.

One caution here: **To wait does not mean to do nothing.** It's good to try out different areas of ministry along the way. Go to conferences. Go to college. Read books that help you. Listen to good people. Talk to pastors, teachers, and people who directly lead ministries. Try working with the homeless, try working with the elderly, try preaching, try mentoring. Waiting is like all those general ed classes everybody is required to take somewhere along the way in college. Some of them may not be what we like, but in the end, it's going to help us get a degree.

Letting the Savior call us means we also seek counsel. The Bible calls this wisdom—and all through the book of Proverbs we're encouraged to look for it and listen to it. I think we've also got to draw from more than one person when we seek counsel. It can't be just one perspective. If we always talk with just one person, it's going to be the same advice over and over.

I believe it's especially important to get wise counsel

from Christians who are older than we are. I talk to my friends all the time, but it's not as if they've been around the block a bunch more than I have. So if I really want meaty advice, I go talk to someone who's got more life experience than I have. One of the people I go to is about eighty years old. She's a great counselor because she's been there. She's seen almost everything there is to see in life, and she's able to give me insight I couldn't get anywhere else.

Sometimes when we wait, the Lord is using that time to heal us. When I was going through my divorce, a family named the Bengards became like a second family to me. Tom, the dad, would phone me up and say: "Hey, we're playing Halo tonight, come on over and hang out with us." Then he'd hang up before I could say no. So I'd come over, we'd shoot pool and play games, his wife would cook good food, and a lot of times I'd end up staying all evening, sometimes spending the night on their couch. Right about that time Tom made me join a bowling league. I was like, "No way, I haven't bowled in years." But it turned out to be so much fun. We had a team name, team shirts, we had a blast—everyone should join a bowling league at least once in their life.

I believe God brought the Bengards into my life at that time to allow me to heal. God wanted me to have a season of rest where I wasn't speaking or writing, where I just went somewhere and allowed God's people to minister to me. Looking back on it now, it was exactly what I needed.

During that time I was looking for another job, and Tom set me straight—"You're a speaker, Ryan," he said. "Stop looking for another job, and start preparing to speak again."

It was counsel I'll never forget.

PART OF HIS PLAN

Abundance comes in so many ways. Sometimes it doesn't seem like we're living the abundant life, but it's really because Christ has called us to wait for a while. And waiting is part of His plan. It may be to strengthen us. It may be to shape and mold us. It may be to allow us a season of restoration or healing. But all that is part of His journey for us, too.

Waiting doesn't mean the Lord has forgotten about us. The exact opposite is true. It means that He cares for us enough to get things right! His aim is that the right events and the right people come along at the right moments. His plan is perfect. His way is *always* good.

If you're in a season of waiting right now, God's call to you today is to not stray from His course. **It might feel terrible, but don't flinch. Don't try to second-guess the One who sees the big picture,** who is Lord over all, and loves you infinitely.

Instead, wait on Him. Choose to love and obey Him. Commit yourself to Him, and you'll find in time that He truly is 2 Live 4.

5

In the Grit

At two in the morning my motorcycle feels cold to the touch. It's all steel and leather, tank and seat, and covered in a layer of dew. The moon is out. The breeze blows in off the unheated ocean with a coolness that runs straight through me.

Outside the motel, my friend Dave has already hit the electric start on his brand-new Yamaha. Same thing with John on his Harley Custom Softail. I'm trying to kick-start my old Triumph, but it's not cooperating. They wait for me, engines idling low and warm, while I push down on my crank again and again. Finally, a cough and a sputter, and my Triumph starts. By then I've broken a sweat and I know once we start moving it will turn icy on my skin.

Minutes later, we're flying, full open-throttle, up Highway 101 through the dark. We've got three hundred and fifty miles to go to reach our destination, and we're focused. The moon looks frosty, the ocean air is wet and cold. I'm switching hands, holding each on my engine until they get warm enough to place back on the handlebars.

I must be doing close to eighty, but as the miles go by Dave and John keep pulling away. Soon I'm thinking they're far ahead of me.

Then I hear a noise that is never good on a moving bike. Silence. Now I'm coasting, rolling without power, pulling off the highway alone in the dark. Of course, eventually Dave and John will realize something's wrong and turn around. But who knows when. It may be hours before help arrives.

I'm alone with a broken bike.

There, on my knees in the gravel by the side of the road, I dig into the engine. I pull the plugs, and sure enough they're fouled. But the bike doesn't start after I clean them. It must be an electrical problem, so I begin to trace wires. Soon I find the culprit—a broken cable. Its housing is brittle, crumbling, an unfixable relic on a bike that was new when Saturday Night Fever first came out.

I stand up to straighten my knees. My hands are black from grease. It's about 3 a.m. and other vehicles are sparse on the highway. Time to face the truth. Even if the guys ride back, my bike isn't going anywhere.

I'm stranded.

Have you noticed? When people tell you about how great it is to ride a motorcycle, they don't tend to bring up times like this.

I've noticed the same thing with a lot of preachers who want you to sell out for Christ. They don't bring up the broken wires and cold gravel parts of the Christian life. That means a lot of young believers think once you become a Christian your struggles are over. You're tapped into the power and strength of an infinite God. He guides. He protects. He's good. Surely that must mean only smooth roads ahead. Right?

Then one night, there you are by the side of the road.

So what's the bare naked truth? When we come to a rough part of our spiritual journey, what do we do?

Is it really possible that the abundant life and broken wires go together?

And for a purpose?

BROKEN WIRES AND COLD GRAVEL

Truth is, Jesus Christ never offered a painless journey. Just look at what His disciples went through. History records that every one of them was eventually persecuted or martyred for their faith. That's something we don't want to hear. Part of being a Christian means going out and celebrating, that's true. But part of being a Christian also means going through hard stuff.

Maybe our struggles take the form of sacrifice. We know we're called to a task, but that means we need to give up something else first. Sacrifice can come in small and big areas. Maybe we're called to volunteer at camp for the summer, but to do so means we need to sell our car to get money for college in the fall. Maybe we're totally into weight training, but to do so means we can't attend a Bible study group we know we need to be at and we have to choose—it's either one or the other.

Maybe our struggles are about disappointment. Disappointment is when we really hope for something, want it, need it…but it doesn't come to pass. Maybe we were really counting on a job to come through, but it didn't. Maybe you and your spouse have been trying to get pregnant for some time, but it's not happening.

Maybe our struggles are about suffering. Maybe your best friend just died of lymphoma and you're just overwhelmed by grief. Or maybe you're completely alone in a new city where you know God wants you to be, but you've felt so lonely and out of it.

At those times, it's easy to wonder: Is this what it means to live the abundant life? Where are You, God? Have You deserted me? Are You still there?

A huge danger at times like this for those who are really living for Him is that you start to slip. Your faith slips. Your personal disciplines slip. **Pretty soon you've slipped back into the "social-hour Christian" mentality.** Hey, God hasn't showed up for you—why should you show up for Him? Before long church turns into a Christmas and Easter thing and you're back to an insurance-policy-against-hell faith.

And there went the abundant life!

Perspective is a good place to start. Though our struggles always feel real to us, it's good to examine them first from a couple different angles. Sometimes everything can fall into place when we check out what we're going through from a larger viewpoint.

It's funny how we read the Bible in North America today. Try as we might, it's hard to study Scripture and apply it to our lives without mixing in our culture's point of view. Like, when we read in Matthew 6:33 that we're to "seek first his kingdom and his righteousness, and all these things will be given to you as well," what comes to mind when we read "all these things?"

Right now, there are Christians in Indonesia who are getting killed for their faith. **I wonder what springs to mind when they read that verse.** Any thoughts?

Right now, there are believers in run-down villages in Haiti who are just hoping they can grow enough food for their families before the next hurricane comes through and washes everything down into the gulley. How might they be reading that verse? Any thoughts?

My aim is not to come down hard on us here, because each culture has its share of problems and temptations. People in America suffer real tragedies too. But for the most part, we're fed and clothed and can worship freely—and those are things not everybody in the world has. So a good place to begin when we struggle is with perspective. While we're praying fervently about which job we should take, there are people praying that their child won't die of malnutrition. Both are important, and worth praying about, but one involves direction, and one involves life or death.

But problems are still real to us. And our call is to go through them. In Matthew 7:13–14 Jesus describes a way of living that leads through a narrow path. "For wide is the gate and broad is the road that leads to destruction, and many enter through it. But small is the gate and narrow the road that leads to life, and only a few find it."

That's us. The narrow gate. Our journey isn't easy.

The abundant life means we'll be out in the battlefields and trenches. Sometimes it's just for a season. Sometimes we'll make our home there.

The abundant life means training and warfare, not traveling down a wide, easy road.

The abundant life means living in the grit of life.

It's an amazing journey with Christ, but it's not always a comfortable one. Being willing to follow Christ means identifying with a Person who suffered. First Peter 4:1 says: "Since Christ suffered in his body, arm yourselves also with the same attitude." The abundant life can mean cold and hurt, isolation and lost friends, being mocked, misunderstood, and more. When people tell you about how great it is to become a Christian, they seldom tell you about that.

But it's the truth.

WITH OUR EYES ON CHRIST

Now for some good news. When we're in the midst of the grit, it's then that God can show up in ways we never imagine. When we're at the end of our rope, Jesus can come in and offer us some surprising answers. Sometimes we see a creative God at work. Sometimes we see the Lord's power. Sometimes we gain a glimpse of resources we never knew existed. Sometimes He gives us no solution at all, but in those times we understand more what it means to live by faith. We understand more of the mystery and wonder of the life He calls us to.

When you follow Christ, life is never boring or dull. It's an adventure. And **a God-sent adventure is nearly always a little or a lot too big for us!** It's usually more than we could grasp with our minds or hold in our hands. Sometimes it's just too much! We really get that when we're kayaking down the Colorado, but do we also get it when we're in the adventure living with Christ?

I love the story from 2 Chronicles 20 where a huge army of bad guys has come to slaughter the people of Judah. Judah's army is completely outnumbered. So Jehoshaphat, the king, arranges a fast for everybody—a time to concentrate in prayer. As all the people come together, Jehoshaphat asks the Lord what they should do.

Can you feel the tension in the scene? It's horrible. All the men of Judah, with their wives and kids, are standing before the Lord. They are silent, expectant, a day or two away from being butchered, robbed, raped, and made slaves. But they are praying. They are awaiting the instruction of God.

As Jehoshaphat cries out to the Lord, he appeals to the Lord on the basis of God's character. *God,* he says—*You rule over all the kingdoms of the nations. Power and might are in Your hands.* Jehoshaphat reminds the Lord of past faithfulness—*O our God, did You not drive out the inhabitants of this land...and give it forever to the descendants of Abraham...?* Jehoshaphat ends his prayer with one phrase that sums up his belief in the character and goodness of God. It shows his absolute dependence, and it shows his absolute faith: *We have no power to face this vast army that is attacking us. We do not know what to do, but our eyes are upon You.*

I love that phrase! "We don't know what to do, but our eyes are on You." That's what it means to live an abundant life! That's the attitude I want to have. Life throws grit and unfixable parts in our path, we don't know what to do...but our eyes are on God. It's His problem now. Our faith in Him gives Him room to go to work.

The Jehoshaphat story's not over. Right then the Lord chooses to speak through the prophet Jahaziel. He stands up in that huge crowd of people and encourages everybody to believe. "Do not be afraid or discouraged because of this vast army," Jahaziel says. "For the battle is not yours, but God's.... You will not have to fight this battle. Take up your positions; stand firm and see the deliverance the Lord will give you."

Do you see God's instruction here? It's not as difficult as the people probably imagined it would be. It's simply this...

Stand still.

The next day dawns bright and clear, and as the army of Judah takes the position God has instructed them to take, to their amazement they find the invading armies have destroyed each other. When Jehoshaphat and all Judah looks over the desert toward the vast enemy armies, they see only dead, rotting bodies all over the ground.

Jesus won the battle. The people only needed the faith to stop, wait, watch, stand still.

Who knew?

APPROACHING A LION

This exhilarating abundant life can be like we're in training, **and our struggles are only there to make us stronger.** Paul talks about this in Philippians 3:13–14. "Straining toward what is ahead," he writes, "I press on toward the goal to win the prize for which God has called me." In other chapters he compares himself to a soldier or an athlete who has gone into strict training to be fit for a definite goal.

So, for a fresh perspective, think for a moment of the abundant life as kind of like doing pushups. I hate pushups. I hate thinking about pushups. I don't feel good while I'm doing them, and I don't feel good when I'm done. I just feel tired and sore. But I keep doing them because there's a payoff in the long run that's better than not feeling sore at the moment.

There's mental training, too. I could never get up there and speak and preach if I wasn't reading and growing and stretching my mind. I read a lot, good stuff, deep stuff— even stuff I don't agree with, because it helps me understand what other people believe. I'm not opposed to hearing other ideas and viewpoints. I love Francis Schaeffer's *How Should We Then Live.* It's a tough book, but I've read it five or six times because I know it's good for my mind. It takes me forever to get through some of the sections, but I keep going. Why? **I'm in training.**

The discipline of fasting enters in here as well. Jesus

fasted. It's definitely taught in the Bible. We should give this some serious thought.

Normally, I eat about ten times a day. It's called grazing, and I think if I were to fast for a couple of days straight, I'd go into shock. In fasting from food, it's best to start small. I have a friend who wanted to do a forty-day fast, like Jesus did. It was his first fast. About eighteen days into it, his parents almost put him in the hospital because he was starting to pass out and say weird things. So start by fasting one meal (after you consult with your doctor, of course). Then one day. Then two. We can also fast from lots of other things besides food. We can fast from TV or the Internet. We can fast from noise. We can fast from business or from a hobby. Times of stillness allow us to know Christ better. Fasting is not always easy, but it's a healthy thing to do.

I hear there are some tribes in Africa where all the young guys need to go out and face a lion in order to be considered a man. In days gone by they had to kill the huge beasts, but with laws protecting wildlife these days, they now just have to **get close enough to a lion to touch it** with a spear.

It's still not an easy thing to do. Imagine it: You've got these thirteen-year-olds approaching a lion up close, giving it a nudge with the pointy end of a spear, then backing off in a hurry without getting themselves chewed on. That may take more courage (or stupidity) than actually killing a lion.

Same with us. Sometimes the struggles in our lives are there so we learn courage, persistence, or how to work out our problems without taking a hike. Life isn't easy. There are lions out there. And we'll probably have to face one some day armed with only a spear.

REAL RIDERS

Back to me with my broken motorcycle and the empty road.

There was nothing to do but wait.

So there's perspective—compared to a world of hunger and global warming, my breakdown wasn't anywhere near as huge. Besides, wherever we're at, in small struggles or big, God can meet us. Sometimes in crazy moments like those, God's presence becomes so real. It's those moments when we pray: "God, I don't know what to do right now, but my eyes are on You." And sometimes He gives direct answers. Sometimes He is quiet, allowing us to develop toughness. Sometimes He gives us the smarts to figure stuff out in ways we may never have dreamed up.

Well, after I did some waiting, God kind of spoke to me out there on the 101. Something like, "You sure you don't know what to do…?"

I had spliced the broken cable together, but with the wrappings all brittle and broken, the wire wasn't insulated anymore, which can prove to be dangerous in a lot of ways. **So I'm chewing gum at the time and suddenly I get this idea:** Why not wrap the broken cable in gum? So I take a few more chews, spit the wad into my hand, wrap the cables, and crank down on the kick-starter.

The bike fires right up, first time. And I rode home—two solid hours—with gum holding my bike together.

I rode it straight to my mechanic's house and showed him the gum job. He brings over another mechanic and they laugh their heads off. But you should have heard the pride in my mechanic's voice.

"Kid!" he says, "I'm proud of you. I knew you had it in you. You're a real rider now, man. You're a real rider."

These days, I don't worry about my old bike holding together so much. Whatever comes, it'll be okay. There'll be a way through.

When we become Christians, it's a little like my bike story.

First we buy a motorbike. Our shiny new faith. It's going to take us all the way there. We've got it, but now we need to ride it.

Then comes the journey. Sometimes it's like roaring up the 101 in the moonlight. But sometimes it's like sitting with our engine in pieces by the side the road. It's dark. We're alone. Major parts are definitely broken.

Then comes perspective. Taken all together, our journey is never boring. It always has a purpose. And it's always in the hands of a God who is good.

That's the adventure Christ promises. That's the abundant life. That's worth living for.

6

The People That Drive Us Nuts

Ever gotten that metallic feeling in the back of your mouth? You've been sitting in class, and whatever the professor is talking about is so far off base that it makes you clench your teeth so hard you can taste your fillings.

I went to a great Christian university, and honestly, 99 percent of the things I was taught there were true and helpful. But I had one teacher who I thought was just wrong—dead wrong—about EVERYTHING! Okay, maybe not everything, but let's say we disagreed about *almost* everything.

I wasn't the type of kid who would just sit there and take it either. I've mellowed out in the past fifteen years. But back then I was known as The Angry Republican. I was on the speech team, I had strong opinions, and my idea of a good time was to take a point and argue it into the ground.

I admit it. I could be a jerk.

So one day, my professor is up there lecturing, and she's

talking about something so completely off in left field that I just couldn't take it anymore. I stood to my feet. I was beyond exasperated. "You can't be serious!" I said, and launched into a tirade about how everything she was saying was illogical, irrational, harmful to society, threatening to life as we know it, and plain, downright stupid.

The speech could have won an Emmy.

But the professor didn't think so. She stopped her lecture. Tears came to her eyes. She ended class on the spot, dismissed everybody, and walked out.

Looking back on it now, I realize how I handled myself that day was embarrassing and inexcusable. Berating someone, especially in public, is never the answer. Even if my ideas were right on, my approach was totally off. I hurt and showed disrespect to somebody. And that was wrong of me.

That's the crazy thing about the Christian life. Sometimes people are complete jerks to us. Sometimes we're complete jerks to them. **People can gnaw away at each other like rats on a block of cheese.** But as followers of Jesus Christ, we're still called to be a community of people. We're not called to walk through the abundant life alone. Other people mold and shape us, even when we disagree with them, they can also sharpen us and hold us accountable.

That's not always easy, especially for strong-minded, independent types.

But it's necessary.

NEVER A PERFECT WORLD

People always talk about how great it was in the early Church. You know that portion of Scripture in Acts 2:42–45 where it talks about how all the believers got along so well? "They devoted themselves to the apostles' teaching and to the fellowship, to the breaking of bread and to prayer. All the believers were together and had everything in common. Selling their possessions and goods, they gave to anyone as he had need. "

Two chapters later, things are still good. "All the believers were one in heart and mind," we read.

Sounds great, doesn't it? But it didn't last long. Almost all of 1 Corinthians is devoted to telling believers how to knock it off and start getting along. And pretty much every letter the apostles wrote to the early church has something in it about settling conflicts, forgiving one another, living in peace—in other words, how to stop being a jerk and start getting along with that jerk next to you.

As soon as you put two people together, even people who love the Lord and claim to believe the same things, you're going to have disagreements, misunderstandings, and problems. People will not always completely understand each other. That's life.

When we're not getting along with non-Christians, sometimes that can be easier for us to handle. I guess we're not surprised when disagreements happen with people whose core outlook is different than ours. But with

Christians, there's a higher expectation. When we become Christians we expect other believers to be nice all the time. But people—*all* people—are different, and people disagree, so it can feel doubly hard.

Here's how this issue relates to the abundant life you and I want so much: When Christians don't get along with other Christians, and the disagreements happen too often, we're extremely vulnerable to questioning the reality of our faith. Or to run away from the relationship. If this is how the followers of Christ act toward one another, something must be wrong with Christianity. Right?

Pretty soon we want nothing to do with the whole thing.

Have you ever heard things like:

- We stopped going to church. People can be so unfriendly there.
- Megan and I used to hang out a lot together, but then she started spreading awful rumors about me. I can't stand her now.
- My old boyfriend said he was a Christian, but he kept pressuring me to do things I didn't want to. Now I don't care what sort of faith a guy has. I just want him to respect me.
- I went to hear this Christian singer once, and he was so arrogant. He had an ego the size of Texas. I'd never go to one of his concerts again.

- We went to our pastor for help, but he didn't do what we asked him to. He barely even listened. That guy's lame. We're outta here.

It's true—when disagreements come up, **a sense of uneasiness lodges itself in our souls.** Sometimes our tempers flare. Sometimes we let loose with words that aren't the kindest. Sometimes we harbor grudges—appearing congenial but cold whenever we see somebody who's wronged us.

Even Paul and Barnabas, two pillars of the faith, didn't get along all the time. In Acts 15:39, we read how they had "such a sharp disagreement that they parted company." Conflicts happen. And they're never easy.

What does conflict have to do with getting more out of life? Sometimes conflicts happen for a reason. They're part of the training ground that causes us to become who we need to be. In Paul and Barnabas' case, their disagreement caused them to go separate directions—Paul took Silas and went to Syria and Cilicia. Barnabas took John Mark and sailed to Cyprus. In doing so, they took the gospel to places it may never have gone so quickly.

A disagreement can be the exact tool that the Lord uses to transform our lives or our situations. It's not that the Lord calls us to purposely go out and have disagreements with other people. Disagreements just happen in the natural course of life. But the Lord, in His goodness and guidance, can use all our interactions with people in His plan for our lives. (Which doesn't mean we're not responsible for how we handle things.)

AN IMPORTANT LOOK—INWARD

When we disagree with people, where's the absolute first place to start? With ourselves. We have to take a good hard look at why we're upset. One of the things people often do is point the blame elsewhere. Even if they were the cause of the disagreement, they'll blame it on how they were raised, or because of some kind of imperfection in their life. **But that's using a crutch. And God never allows us to do that.**

I've been diagnosed with Attention Deficit Disorder. And it's affected my ability to get along with various people throughout my lifetime. But so what. It's totally *my* responsibility to learn how to live with it. To even see it as a benefit—something that will help my life and ministry.

It wasn't always that way. I wasn't diagnosed with A.D.D. until I was in my early twenties. If you don't have it, it's almost impossible to describe what it's like. When I was a kid I simply could not sit still. Classroom desks were like a jail sentence to me. It's like I almost had no control over my need to stand, or to move around and get rid of excess energy.

Teachers were much less informed on how to handle it back then. I had one who used masking tape to keep me in my chair. Didn't work. In junior high I was suspended for talking too much in class. I just had to be saying something, going somewhere, all the time. In college, my A.D.D. exhibited itself in an inability to concentrate on any one thing. After I was diagnosed, I took the drug Ritalin for a while, and I could concentrate like crazy. Guys would never want to play video games with me when I was taking Ritalin because I'd never lose focus. I mean never. Even better, my grades went up a full letter. I'm not on Ritalin anymore. I decided this was me, A.D.D. and all, and I was going to learn to succeed with the challenges I've got.

Today, I think my A.D.D. actually helps fuel me. My personality is that I'm always on the go. I think fast. I move fast. It's hard for me to sit still. Yet, the Lord is using that in my life. I keep a quick schedule. I speak all over the country. I'm not the type of guy who is called to sit all day behind a computer. Nothing wrong with that—it's just not me.

Here's the hard word, you may not want to hear it, but it's the truth: If you've had a difficult childhood, then I'm genuinely sorry you were raised that way. But it absolutely does not give you an excuse to lower your standards now. I know there's such a thing as being a victim too. If you were hurt in your past and it still comes up in your life now and causes problems, then I'm also sorry for what you had to go through. But **you can't use that as an excuse to blow it now.** Whatever your situation is, whatever your disadvantage or limitation, it can't be used as a crutch. We've all got to be responsible for ourselves, no matter what kind of cards we were dealt in life.

I have a good friend who had a very rough childhood—I mean a seriously tragic family life. Grandparents raised him because his parents were on drugs and drank too much. A car hit his mom just over a year ago. At the time of the accident she was a prostitute. She was crossing a street when she was hit. His dad is almost blind and deaf due to advanced diabetes believed to be caused from years of substance abuse.

But today my friend has managed to rise above the poor examples and upbringing he received growing up. He's an exception to the rule of what people tend to believe. He is an outstanding teacher and coach. He affects kids' lives in a positive way and helps them grow into healthy young adults. I've spent time with the kids he teaches and I've seen firsthand the difference he's made in their lives. Here's the scary thing—I bet if he had chosen to, he could have behaved any way he wanted. He could have robbed, murdered, and raped and then said, "But look how I was raised," and everybody would go, "Yeah, what a shame, but it's totally understandable."

My friend has overcome his past because he's chosen to take responsibility for himself.

And that's what we all need to do.

Shouldering responsibility means knowing where we struggle. It's being genuine and honest about who we are and what our weak points are, knowing what we need to do to get on track and stay there…then making the necessary choices to do so.

With my own life, **I've had to work on my bluntness—just ask the professor I reduced to tears.** I know now that my harshness with her communicated a lack of respect. Christ's call on my life is not to beat people over the heads with my desire or ability to debate. It's to love them and care for them.

I wrote a bestselling book a couple of years back called *Be Intolerant* about the importance of taking a stand for what's right. But if I could go back and clarify anything about it today, I'd tell people that in no way was that book a call to be insensitive and obnoxious. It wasn't even a call to arms. It wasn't written to drum up some sort of modern Crusader movement where Christians confront all moral relativists and tell them they're stupid. It was about loving people enough to talk to them about their lives—especially when you know they're heading down the wrong path. It was also written for Christians to examine their own lives to see if they've fallen for any of the traps of moral relativism. But the point was not to call people names or be harsh with them. It was to have courage of conviction.

WHY WE NEED EACH OTHER

Once we take responsibility for our own actions, the transforming work that God has for our lives can really begin.

God molds and shapes us into who He wants us to be using the power of the Holy Spirit and our own resources. One of the most helpful tools in this area is accountability.

Sometimes we think of accountability as simply someone who we go to when we mess up. Like, if a guy is trying to be sexually pure with his girlfriend, he'll get an "accountability partner"—someone who can ask him if purity is happening.

That may be one definition of accountability—but I want to broaden it here. **Accountability is when we have people in our lives who know us, our strengths and weaknesses, and they care enough to walk through the situations of life with us.** We need people like this. Accountability means we have other people in our lives we answer to. We have people that can ask us all the hard questions they can think of and confront us with the truth when we're off track. They also pray for us, notice areas of our life we may need help in, and help us smooth off the rough areas of our personality. Accountability helps guard us from harm. It's one of the most courageous relationships we can set up. Accountability is close to the same thing as discipleship in that it's meeting with another person on a regular basis to help us grow more like Christ.

Anytime we meet someone who drives us nuts, we need to bring in another person who helps us figure out the situation, the person that holds us accountable in this area.

It may be that the accountability person says: "Yeah, well the other guy is being a jerk, and here's how you can talk to him instead of yelling at him." Or it may be that that person says, "Actually, that's how life works sometimes, and really, that guy isn't being a jerk—he just has a different way of doing things than you do—so you need to back off." Accountability and wisdom go hand in hand.

But let me give you a picture instead of more words.

I recently watched a show about tow-in surfing. It's called "tow-in" because you've got straps on your surfboard and a jet-ski tows you out into the big waves you could never paddle into. There's a competition for the biggest wave surfed, and the prize is $1,000 for every foot. So there's this guy surfing a huge sixty-five-foot wave, and he gets a check for $65,000.

When this guy got this award, he said, "I wouldn't be here if it wasn't for so and so"—and here he named his tow-in guy. And, "This isn't just about me, this is about both of us." This is fairly common, I've seen it before—some surfers even split the proceeds with their tow-in.

That's a picture of accountability. **Someone's looking out for you, someone you depend on, someone you rely on to help keep you safe.** Proverbs 27:17 says "As iron sharpens iron, so one man sharpens another." We could not be who God wants us to be without other people in our lives. People who raise issues in the form of disagreements, and accountability partners who help us work through those issues.

CHANGE HAPPENS

A couple of semesters after I had the run-in with the professor, I had another disagreement with another teacher. I had chosen not to do an assignment outside of class that I thought would be harmful to the name of Christ in that area of the city, and my grade took a huge hit. I could have fought the grade. I could have ranted and railed and taken it to the dean of students. But this time I didn't. I just took the F, and I took the class over again.

I'm not sure I knew it at the time, but looking back on it now I'd say, "Yeah, that's abundant living." **I was learning that I could be right, and gentle too.** Honestly, I'd have never made progress on that issue without having to deal with people whose viewpoints pushed all my buttons.

How about you? Who is that one person—or maybe it's a group of people—who can drive you nuts? How do you typically respond to that person? Does that response go hand-in-hand with the kind of person Christ is calling you to be?

Could it be that the person in your life who is rattling your cage is there for a reason? God doesn't want you to run away from this, He wants you to grow through it. Once you take responsibility for your actions and seek other people to help you work through the issues involved in it, then you're on your way to changing, with the help of the Holy Spirit's power in your life.

The insane truth is this: The most unlikely events and most irritating people are part of the abundant life! Why? Because it's those very people and events that Christ uses to show us things we might not see otherwise. He wants us to see the truth, live the truth, and change.

God is good.
His way is perfect.

Our call is to trust Him to lead us forward into more and more of the full, authentic life He wants for each of us.

7

One Day She Made a Choice

I don't know her name, where she lived, or much about her at all. But one day when she was a teenager, she made a choice, and because of that choice, I'm here today.

I think about her sometimes. I owe her a lot. In my heart, she stands for courage. And that's why she comes to mind first in this chapter about courage in the big and small...

The jet had just leveled off. The earth had disappeared into a cloudbank thousands of feet below. I was flying home from Costa Rica. I'd been down there on a surf trip—it had nothing to do with missions. It was a vacation. A personal adventure trip. It was just my time to get away and see a piece of the planet I had always wanted to.

I was just about to put on my headphones, close my eyes and remember in dreamland the most incredible surf I had ever experienced in my life, when I heard the guy sitting next to me say something.

"Are you a pro surfer?"

I pretended I didn't hear him. But the question came again. "Hey, are you a pro surfer?"

Okay, the guy's question was legitimate. I looked like a surfer. The week before I had dyed my hair fluorescent green—bright as a neon sign. I had on camo shorts, flip-flops, and a T-shirt.

But "no" was all I said. I hoped the one-word answer would give him the hint.

"What do you do then?" he asked. He just wasn't going to give up. I had to spill the beans.

"I'm a writer and a speaker."

"What do you write about?"

"Christianity and faith," I said. But I was still thinking about getting those headphones on.

It's a funny thing about the conversations you can have on airplanes. It's like walls that are normally there are down when you're sitting next to someone for a couple hours. Complete strangers totally open up.

That's what this guy was about to do. "You know, I really needed to hear that," he said. Then he choked up and got a bit teary. I could tell he wanted to talk more.

But I was exhausted from the trip and let it drop. We said a few more things between us, but nothing substantial. Soon I put my headphones on and went to sleep.

You know how I feel about that experience now? I blew

it. Big time. I'm embarrassed and convicted about it. It's like I was totally given an opportunity to talk to someone about Jesus Christ, and I failed. Here's my calling: Every time someone says, "What do you do?" —that's when I'm supposed to give a truthful answer. I'm not responsible for how the person responds. I'm only responsible for being faithful to my call. What I say could be as simple as: "I'm a speaker. I talk about Jesus."

That's what I'm supposed to be doing, but sometimes it makes me feel nervous or inadequate. Or I think the other person will think I'm a freak.

That's where courage is required. Courage to follow God, **even in the small choices we face every day.** Because it's out of those small areas of obedience that God wants to raise up a huge life for us.

IT'S ALL IMPORTANT

People talk about God's will for their lives in big areas all the time. It's like, *I wonder where God wants me to go to college, I wonder who God wants me to marry, I wonder what sort of occupation I should have.* I'm not knocking that. The Lord is concerned about every area of our lives, and His promise is to guide us and give us wisdom in all areas.

But are the same people who are so concerned about God's will in big areas just as concerned about God's will in small areas? Are you? Am I?

The small choices are unbelievably important.

Small things have a way of leading into big areas, but they're also important because life is made up of a lot of small moments.

God's will in small areas could be as simple as:

- How polite (or not) we are to the girl behind the checkout counter.
- How long we stay on one channel (or don't) when we're flipping back and forth between TV shows.
- How close we get when we're following another car on the freeway—and why we feel we need to get as close as we do.
- The figures we write down (or don't write down) when filling out our tax returns.
- The jokes we laugh at (or don't laugh at) in the lunchroom at work.
- What we choose to wear (or don't wear) when we go out on a date.

Sometimes people are convinced the Lord is setting them up for huge things and I say, "maybe, maybe not." Maybe He will want you to do something huge someday, but maybe that day is a long way off because He wants you to prove yourself trustworthy in the small things yet. Even if we don't get to do those bigger things someday, it's still worth it in the long run to do the small things right.

That's why courage is so important. Not just the fight-a-lion type of courage, but courage to have integrity in the small stuff. The stuff no one else knows about, and never will. Courage means we're bold. We risk. We care more about being true than what people think. The bottom line in our lives becomes doing what we're supposed to do—end of story.

What if we've got a long string of failures in our past? Is it ever too late to have integrity be a part of our life?

I believe that **character means we move beyond our failures.** If we mess up, we can't beat ourselves down with how we blew it. We've got to keep going. Are we embarrassed? Are we convicted? Good. Own it, confess it, and don't blow it again next time. My dad has always said: "It's never wrong to do what's right. It's never right to do what's wrong." So whatever happened yesterday, we have to face it, own it, repent of it…and move on.

There are two great verses in this area: The first is 1 John 1:9—"If we confess our sin, he is faithful and just to forgive us our sins and purify us from all unrighteousness." That means His grace is always available. His arms are always open to us when we come to Him. We will never mess up to the extent that God's love and forgiveness become unavailable to us.

The second verse is Isaiah 1:18—"'Come now, let us

reason together,' says the LORD. 'Though your sins are like scarlet, they shall be as white as snow; though they are red as crimson, they shall be like wool.'" This means that God can totally transform our lives, no matter where we've been, no matter what we've done.

His power is that big. His love for us is that wide.

THE WHOLE OBEDIENCE THING

I want to talk more about obedience, because that's what following Christ in the small and big areas of life is really about. Sometimes the line between small areas and big areas gets blurry. Like His call to love other people. Is that a big area or a small area? Really, it can be both. So the issue for us when we live the abundant life boils down to obedience. Will we follow Jesus no matter what the cost?

Obedience is something we don't get excited about very often. Obedience means we follow commands. That's not the easiest thing to do. Have you ever watched a mom telling her kid to keep her voice down indoors, to not run out in the street, to not draw on walls—or any of the hundreds of other commands any parent will need to give a kid? Obedience is not something we naturally do when we're kids, and it's not always the path we follow when we're grown up either.

There's something in all of us that doesn't like to be told what to do, even though we know it's good for us. The apostle Paul expresses this struggle so perfectly in Romans 7:15. He admits he has no idea why he keeps messing up all the time—he just keeps doing so. "I do not understand what I do," he writes. "For what I want to do I do not do, but what I hate I do."

Can you relate?

God knows obedience is difficult. Still, He tells us to walk in paths that are good and not harmful. He knows that if certain promises are obeyed, the results can help produce an amazing life. God also knows that if certain promises are disobeyed, the results can hurt us.

Think for a moment. What happens when we disobey God?

- Bad stuff carries harmful consequences. We do bad stuff and we get into trouble or hurt. It's as simple as that.
- It doesn't feel good to disobey. Not really. When we're out of line, it may feel like a buzz for the moment, but afterwards comes stress, fear, or embarrassment.
- We can't respect ourselves when we sin. It's impossible.
- If we're blowing it, we don't want to go to church or hang out with other Christians much.
- None of our friendships run as smooth.

• This can lead to great times of loneliness when the guilt and shame cause us to pull back from friends.

God's will for you and me is to obey Him so that He can open up the full extent of His blessings for us. Yes, God always loves us, even when we sin. When we sin, God's arms are still open wide to us. But when we repent and choose to obey Him—when we fully follow His pathways wholeheartedly—we are able to have the full relationship with Him that we want. We are able to have the amazing lives He fully intends for us to have.

Joshua 24:14–15 records a classic struggle between wavering and obedience. "Now fear the LORD and serve Him with all faithfulness," Joshua instructs the Israelites. "But if serving the Lord seems undesirable to you, then choose for yourselves this day whom you will serve."

Can you hear the words of Joshua in your ear today? "Choose for yourself whom you will serve." It's easy to hesitate when it comes to sin. We know what to do, or what not to do. The truth lies before us, but we're still indecisive.

Courage. That's what it's all about.

Courage to follow the Lord no matter how big or small an area is. God's call for us is to do what's right. **Every time.** Even the time after the time we did it wrong.

COURAGE IS A CHOICE

Remember the teenage girl I mentioned at the beginning of this chapter? I am the direct result of someone doing the right thing after doing the wrong thing. In a way, I owe my whole existence to her obedience. I would not be here today if she hadn't had the courage to change course after getting it wrong, and doing what was right.

That person was my biological mother.

Like I said, I don't know her name or where she lived. She was seventeen years old when she got pregnant, and she wasn't married. About my biological dad, I know next to nothing.

My biological mother was one of five brothers and sisters, so her parents weren't into raising another kid. She had a decision to make. These days there'd be a good chance I'd be aborted. I'm sure that horrible route was presented to her back then, too. But she went to an adoption agency instead. And when I was six weeks old, the agency placed me with Jim and Shirley Dobson.

Even though we've never tried to hide this, not a lot of people know that about my family. My sister, Danae, is my parents' biological child. After my parents had her, my mom wasn't able to get pregnant again. My folks knew they wanted to have another child. That's when I came along.

It's funny, because people tell me all the time I look like my dad, Jim Dobson. Or they'll come up to me and say—"Oh, I see so much of your mom in you," (meaning

Shirley). That's okay. I consider both those statements compliments. They are my true parents. I'm not looking for any other ones.

My parents never hid from me the fact I was adopted. **They always told me I was wanted and loved and that God sent me to them in a special way.** When I was a kid, I never understood it completely, but being adopted has never bothered me. Ever.

Today when I think about my biological mother, I feel thankfulness. There are plenty of single parents out there who are really exceptional parents—they totally sacrifice all the time for their children. But there hasn't been a study yet that suggests that children raised in one-parent families do better than those raised with two parents. I don't mean that to sound harsh. Many single moms do wonderfully. Then there are two-parent families who completely blow it. But when a biological mother in really bad circumstances gives up her child so the kid can be raised by two other loving parents—well, that can be the most sacrificial love anyone can have for a child.

Especially if, like me, you're that child looking back on a blessed life.

My biological mother did the right thing. I can't imagine what she must have gone through, or how hard that was to give up her baby. I'm sure there are times when she wonders if she did the right thing. She did. I'm incredibly grateful she did so. Courage is a choice. She could have chosen something easier. But she chose to do the right thing.

BETWEEN WAVES

I know this guy, he's a good guy, and he's been struggling for some time, trying to figure out this whole Christianity thing.

So we're out surfing one day, and he paddled up and asked me about Christ. It was a bold move on his part, and this time I just jumped on it, since he had asked some good questions and I was feeling bolder than I did that day when I was on the plane. He didn't give his life to Christ right there or anything, but I think he's a lot closer to knowing the truth.

We talked about his spiritual quest a long time out there in the water. Between waves, of course. There's a funny thing about surfers. Surfers talk out in the water all the time. Sometimes as we're talking, we'll be in the middle of a sentence, with the whole conversation left hanging, and we'll turn to catch a wave and start paddling like mad. Then afterwards we'll paddle back and pick up exactly where we left off, right in the middle of something serious.

Following Christ can be like that. It comes in bits and pieces. There's a small area of obedience here, a small instance of following Him there, a conversation here, a conversation there. Then there are huge events. The big waves come and it's our decision to catch them or not. Then we paddle back out and go back to our conversations. Big areas. Small areas. **Christ's call is to follow Him, no matter what the situation is.**

When you take a good honest look at your life, how obedient are you to Christ? Have you committed to doing the right thing, no matter what the cost? **What small choice are you facing today that could change a life—maybe yours—for years to come?**

Jesus Christ is a God of grace. He's not hanging over us with a big stick, threatening to whack us when we get out of line. But He still calls us to obey His commands. In the small choices too.

It's for our sake. And it's all part of this amazing road trip into the abundant life He has for us.

8

Just Preach It

Here's something you and I have in common with
Billy Graham and Mother Teresa: Our job description
while we're on earth—if we're followers of Jesus Christ—is
to preach the gospel by what we say and do at all times and
in all places.

You thought preaching was just for preachers? The job
of the reverend up front—the guy with the smooth talk
and the nice clothes?

If so, then you're only halfway to real living. That kind
of living means that preaching is what you do, who you
are. No exceptions.

**I'll admit, "preach" is a word that
most of us don't use every day.** I mean, it's
not like everybody gets up, eats breakfast and thinks: "*All
right!* I get to preach today!" Because "preach" is kind of an
in-your-face type of word. Few of us actually think of ourselves as preachers.

But one way or another, we're all called to share our
faith. To spread the news of new life in Christ, even on our

bad days. Even on the days when we try and fail…badly.

A few years ago I had the opportunity to tour with a couple of bands as their MC and speaker. A bunch of times on that tour it went really bad when I preached. And I don't mean a little bad, I mean people throwing stuff bad. No fun.

But in a way, I understand. People usually come to concerts to hear music, not to listen to some guy they don't know or care about deliver a speech.

So picture this: The bands play, and everybody's absolutely rocking out, and then…Ryan gets up to speak. *Ryan who? Ryan why?* The audience just wants to get back to the music!

What happens next? Everyone thinks this is the time to go out and get a soda or go to the bathroom or something. **There I am preaching my heart out to an empty room,** and I'm thinking: *Should I even be here?*

I'm not saying it's always like that—or even usually. I love it when God uses me to hold an auditorium full of teenagers in rapt attention for an hour and a half. But it's not always that exciting.

I've had people heckle me, boo me, yell at me, throw stuff and scream out loud at inappropriate times in the middle of my talks. I've argued with God before—"Please let me just tell some funny stories and get out of here!" But God reminds me: "No, you've got to preach the gospel. That's the only reason you're up there in the first place."

So I keep going.

Once, while speaking at a school, three guys in the front row talked the whole time I was up there. And they were loud. And nobody shut them up. I've never felt it's been my call to manage anybody from the stage. So I just kept on going. I didn't know what else to do. But I figured, well, at least it's only three guys talking. I've still got 297 people listening. So that's not too bad.

Do you want an abundant life with Jesus Christ? You gotta preach! And preaching isn't easy. But you gotta preach.

OPEN YOUR EYES

Fortunately, preaching is not all hard times. There are times when I stand up and the crowd becomes absolutely silent, and they totally listen. And it's as though God has chosen that moment for some reason to do an amazing work in people's hearts. At moments like those I remind myself that this is my calling. This is what God wants me to do. I'm a preacher. *Thank You, Lord, for the honor and privilege.*

And you know what? **It's your honor and privilege, too.** Jesus asked and expected all of His followers to spread the good news of the gospel. Insurance policy Christians might be happy that they're going to heaven when they die, and leave it at that. But 2 Live 4 Christians know better. There's work to be done right here right now, work that's waiting for you and me to do. People

are lost and going to hell, they're in misery and they need
to know that God loves them and saves them through the
work Christ did on the cross. And there are people around
us each day that only you and I will have the opportunity
to preach to. Appointments for God, conversations, challenges that are on our schedule for the day—and no one
else's.

Jesus said it like this in John 4:35: **"Open your
eyes and look at the fields! They are
ripe for harvest."** It was a metaphor that Jesus was
using—a picture that meant: *Get out there and preach.*

A COUPLE THINGS PREACHING ISN'T

Part of the problem is that people read all those verses
about preaching and then get stupid. I mean, there's all
sorts of ways people can preach—and you never know
which one God is going to use to reach people. So I don't
want to knock anybody here, but people can be complete
jerks about sharing their faith.

There are a couple things I've learned along the way:
Other people are never "argued" into the kingdom of God;
it's tough to bash people over the head with a Bible and
have them respond well; it's hard to share Christ with
someone and not care about them; and if you're going to
preach your life has got to be in line with Christ's teach-
ings—otherwise Christianity comes across as hypocritical
and irrelevant.

But another problem is that people use all these reasons and more as an excuse not to share their faith. How many times have you heard things like:

- I'd share my faith, but I just don't know what to say.
- People have a right to believe anything they want. There's no way I'd impose my beliefs on someone else.
- I'm just not into evangelism. It's not my spiritual gift. That's my pastor's job.
- I'm too shy.
- My life's a mess right now.
- I'm too tired to talk about God right now (like me on the plane coming back from Costa Rica).

The message of Jesus Christ is not dependent on the state or quality of your life. Christ saved me while I was still a sinner. To *receive* His salvation, I had to repent of my sins and respond to Him. That was my part. If I had to stop sinning just to *hear* the message of Christ, I'd still be on my way to hell. So when I preach the gospel I say: "If you're a sinner, okay. That's who Jesus came to save. You can be a drug addict and become a Christian. You can be a pornographer and become a Christian. You can be a homosexual and become a Christian."

It's up to the Holy Spirit, not me, to come into people's lives with the power and authority to change those things or anything else He wants to change about a person.

THE SIMPLE TRUTH

What is the gospel truly all about?

Really, it's just about bad news and good news. The bad news is that we were all born sinners. God is a holy God and can't have anything to do with sin, so we're separated from Him. The good news is that Jesus Christ provided a way to God when Christ died on the cross. Jesus offers us a gift, and it's our choice to repent of our sins and receive it. A whole new life—now and in eternity—starts right there.

That's the Gospel.

It can get more complex than that—but not really. You don't have to remember much more than that about the core of Christ's message. Think of the verse that so many people learn when they're kids—John 3:16: "For God so loved the world that he gave his only Son, that whoever believes in him shall not perish but have eternal life." That's the gospel.

Preaching is our call as believers. We're all called to talk about our faith. It can be scary. It can feel ineffective. But this is what the life worth living is all about. It's being there and caring for people and showing them what and who Jesus Christ is all about.

IF NECESSARY, USE WORDS

I think it was St. Augustine who said: "Preach the gospel at all times. If necessary, use words."

I love that. It allows us to be ourselves. It allows us to be real. It allows us to be authentic. But it still tells us to get out there and preach. So maybe it was like Augustine was saying: "Don't get hung up on the word *preach*. You don't always have to talk to show people the love of Jesus Christ. Just get out there and be you, and when you love people and your love for the Lord shows through, your preaching will just flow."

When I say "get out there and preach," I don't mean that everybody should have a ministry where they stand up in front of people with a microphone. Think of preaching as communicating the ministry of Jesus Christ. Communication happens a lot of different ways. But **it's always about a Person—Christ.** What is Jesus all about? What is He truly here for? Then, how can we communicate that to those people we meet and know? That's preaching.

My friend Zack is a preacher, although he'd probably never say he was. He's just a really solid guy who consistently does the right thing. He had this really crummy job—I mean *really*—where his boss totally overworked all his employees and walked around screaming at people. Once, Zack's boss fired three people, then he gave Zack a dollar raise and loaded the work of those three people on him.

So I used to phone Zack just to bug him, and I'd say things like: "Dude, we're totally going surfing today. You gotta ditch work and come with us." I was just trying to yank his chain. But I was a bit serious too. I mean, that guy had a horrible job, and sometimes you just need a break. But Zack never would. I guess to go surfing he would have had to phone in sick, and he felt that would be dishonest. And he wouldn't do it.

That says a lot. Zack's character was consistently honorable. He wanted to do right no matter what. I don't know who noticed that and who didn't. But his choice made me reexamine my own life. And that's preaching. It's communicating the message of Christ without words.

Another friend of mine, Annie, is the world's most creative person. Once, she agreed to help set up this event, and she totally went all out for it. She made personalized napkins, luggage tags, all this stuff—she'd find out exactly what a person needed and then provide it. Her thoughtfulness spoke volumes to a crowd of people that day. I don't exactly know how the Holy Spirit uses stuff like that to open people's hearts, but I know that Annie is a person who "preaches" all the time without using words—the love of Christ just shows so vividly in her life.

We have to be careful, though. Good works in Christ's name doesn't exactly equal preaching the gospel. It's only part of it. After all, you and I know a lot of thoughtful, responsible, hard-working people who do not follow Christ. That's why in every case possible, **you and I need to be ready to say the words of life—just speak them out—and ask God to bless them, no matter how much we stumble and stutter around.**

I'M JUST THE GUY WHO BOMBED

One great thing about preaching is that we're never responsible for how people respond. Our call is to preach, not to get people to make decisions. There's this totally cool thing about God's character. He's sovereign. That just means He's in control of things. He reigns supreme over all. He doesn't ask us to change people. That's His job. He just asks us to be faithful, to speak the truth for Him in our world, to be willing to share the gospel however we know how.

Whether people respond or not is up to Him. I've given talks before where I'm sweating it, I get up and speak, and I seem to bomb. Then when I invite people to come forward to find out more about Christ, nobody comes.

Is that encouraging? No. Is it okay? Yes. For one thing, I can't see inside. I never truly know who responded and who didn't. Maybe somebody did. Maybe nobody did. For another, the results are not my responsibility. They're God's. **My responsibility is to faithfully speak for Him to the very best of my ability.**

Then again, who really knows how the Holy Spirit works? Sometimes when we think nothing is happening, really, everything is happening. We just don't know it yet. Once I was speaking outdoors and the weather was absolutely freezing. I got up on stage and just went for it— I mean, I'm throwing my A-game out there. I'm trying to warm the crowd up, telling jokes, dancing, singing—whatever it takes. But nobody's clapping. They're not laughing. They're not even smiling. I mean, it was terrible.

So I presented the gospel, got off stage in a hurry and just hung my head. The security guard who travels with us is backstage, and I'm like: "Dude, I bombed.

He says, "No way man, that was one of your best times ever."

And I go: "What are you talking about? Didn't you see the crowd? They were totally dead."

He goes, "Ryan, they weren't dead. They're frozen! It's just too cold outside to move!"

He wasn't kidding. Just before the event started, there had been ice on the seats. They had to chip ice away to have people be able to sit down.

I think the Holy Spirit used that time to remind me it's never about me. It's never about my read on the situation. It's about Him. He is the One who's at work. He is the One who totally changes hearts and lives.

My part is to get up there and preach it.

"IT'S NOT ABOUT YOU"

One time I'm up speaking and, this time, the auditorium is totally blazing. Everybody's just sweating and the lights are hot up front, and I'm just totally going for it in spite of the heat. And I preach, and I get done, and I give an altar call.

And not one person comes forward. Dead silence. Nothing.

And I think, *All right*, and I step off the stage.

Next a drama team gets up, and they do this horribly cheesy staged production. It was so canned. It was horrible. And I'm just watching it from backstage just thinking that the night has gone from bad to worse.

But we're not done. A new guy gets up and starts giving a short version of my message—just summarizing stories I'd given and stuff. He's like: "When Ryan said this…" and "Ryan made a good point when he said such and such…" and he's redoing my speech. And you know what? His sermon on my sermon was turning out a lot better. That was humbling.

Then he tells everyone, "You know, if you want to believe in the Jesus that Ryan just preached about, and you want to come and know the Lord, then you should come forward."

This time, people came forward. By the hundreds. I mean it. It's like wave after wave of people pour out of the audience. And they're crying. And they're praying. **And they're accepting the Lord for the first time in their lives.**

Me? I'm speechless. I want to run away and give my speaker's fee back and say, "I'm sorry for even showing up, you shouldn't have ever had me, I'm a terrible speaker and I never want to do this again."

But as I sat there watching all those people come forward, it was like the Holy Spirit said to me: "You see, you big idiot, it's not about you. If I want people to come and know Me, *I'll* touch their hearts. I just want you to get up and do what I ask you to do."

That's what this amazing life is all about. It's not about what we do. It's about Who we know. And He's indescribable. It's wilder than we could ever imagine.

FEELS LIKE SURFING

What does speaking out for Jesus Christ feel like? Let me think. If you have never surfed, I could never tell you exactly what it's like. I can't describe to you the feeling of paddling out in frigid cold water and watching and waiting and feeling that surge of a huge wave and paddling like mad to catch it and pushing off a board and standing up in a crouch and making a bottom turn and barely holding it under control and riding it out with white water at your back...then turning around and doing it all again and again.

I can't describe it to you. You have to experience it. You have to jump in the water for yourself and get wet. But maybe I could describe it in a way that makes you want to experience it.

That's what preaching is like. That's my goal. I want to describe the Christian life in a way that makes people want to take that first leap. I want to introduce them to a Person who's indescribable. You just have to know Him for yourself.

And you know what? In spite of me, people come to

know Jesus. In spite of how stupid I can be. In spite of the fact I'm a sinner. People still come to know Him.

People get to experience the amazing life Christ offers right here, right now, and then they get to experience it for all eternity.

That's a message 2 Live 4.

9

Open Throttle Here

Have you seen the movie *Dodgeball?* I can't recommend it because there's a lot of junk in it, but it's about a group of misfits who enter a dodgeball tournament in order to save their cherished gym from the onslaught of a corporate fitness chain.

Okay. **I just copied that last sentence word-for-word** from a movie promo site. I hope they don't sue me for plagiarism.

Anyway, in the extra features section of the DVD, the director, Rawson Marshall Thurber, tells how he got in a scrap with the studio because he wanted to have a sad ending, and they insisted on a happy one.

Forget happy. Thurber believes that in a real game of dodgeball, the misfits would have lost because that's what usually happens on school playgrounds across America. That's how he shot the first ending.

But the studio made him change it to show the misfits beating the tough guys instead. Unrealistic maybe, but that's what people want, and that's what sells tickets. So the happy ending stayed. Studio's orders.

What's a life worth living for, anyway? Surely in a book like mine that's trying to understand the real, abundant life that Jesus promises we should expect happy endings too. Wouldn't that be Studio's orders?

Well, maybe. But let's hang on and look for the truth.

A JOURNEY, NOT AN ENDING

The truth is, happy endings are what we long for, but they can become dangerous if we insist on them at the expense of reality—at the expense of living right now.

I'm not telling people to forget about heaven. Never.

Heaven is the true happy ending that's guaranteed.

The Bible tells us that heaven is a reward worth looking forward to, and to keep our goal on the life to come. But that's not the happy ending I'm talking about.

What I want to shake you free from is camping on the false "happy ending" of becoming a Christian. Conversion can be a happy experience, absolutely. But it's definitely not an "ending." It's just the best place to start.

It's the biggest, most powerful ride you can imagine, the one you've been waiting for. God brought you here—

no doubt about it. But now you have to get on and open the throttle…and hang on for the run of your life!

God has an important and unforgettable journey ahead with your name written all over it.

Unfortunately, too many Christians look at when they accepted Christ as their finish line—not their starting line. To them, their conversion is the completion of their lives, not the beginning. And right now, they're stuck at that conversion point—mindlessly staying put in the moment, the "happy ending" of accepting Christ—and that moment only. *Why do anything else?* they wonder—*I've got my insurance policy. I'm set.*

But that's fake. That's movie-set Christianity—not the whole picture. And it's keeping a lot of "church" people from the wild, free, world-changing life God offers.

Instead, Christ calls us to accept Him, then *live* for Him. This new-life-in-the-present adventure with Jesus Christ is the abundant life God offers us. It's not just a happy ending midpoint in our lives, a moment to remember. Not hardly. It's the happy beginning of another whole story that's just begun! A story that is entirely taken up with knowing, obeying, and becoming like this supreme **Someone who truly is 2 Live 4.**

When Christians focus only on the "happy ending" of when they became a believer, it's easy to get lost in the reality of life. Trials come, or God asks us to wait, or we get hurt, or we wonder what to do in life—all those things go into living the life that Christ calls us to right now. That's part of the amazing journey. If we're stuck on the happy ending, we never know the depths of the wonders of God.

In Philippians 4:13 the apostle Paul says: "I can do everything through him who gives me strength." Think about that! Do you and I truly believe that for our own lives? Paul doesn't just say "some things," he says "everything." That's what Christ offers us. **Everything!** We can do *everything* through Him! What this looks like will be different for different people. God doesn't call us all to the same thing. But there is an amazing, completely unbelievable life available to us, when we truly walk through life with Christ.

Let me tell you one last story to show what I think this kind of life can look like.

ON AN EVENING IN JUNE

When you hit rock bottom in your life, somewhere in there you've got to make a decision to keep going. A couple years ago, I did that. As part of my rebuilding process, I started dating again.

But—maybe you already know this—after you reach a certain age, dating is seldom actually fun. It's evaluation time. You're sizing the other person up, and they're doing the same to you. It's the ultimate interview.

So I was dating this one girl, and it didn't work out. So we broke up, and I started dating someone else, but it wasn't going very well. Somewhere in the midst of that, the first girl sent me an e-mail, just as a friend this time, telling me she had found the perfect girl for me. My first thought was, *That's kind of weird. Why is she sending me this?* and I think I deleted the e-mail without responding.

About four or five months went by and another friend asked me if I had ever met the girl that my former girlfriend had e-mailed me about. My friend said, "Yeah, she's perfect for you. She surfs. She's spunky. She loves the Lord and is into youth ministry."

So I thought, "Well, if two people are saying the same thing, I'll give it a shot." I sent this girl, whose name is Laura, an e-mail. We talked on the phone once or twice, but it was no big thing. She was actively dating as well. We were both keeping busy lives. We even tried to meet a couple of times, but nothing worked out. We always just missed each other by like five minutes or something. Once, we were supposed to meet at this surf competition. We were both there, about fifty feet away from each other we figured out later, but by the time she got to where I was, I had left.

On the day after I moved into my new apartment—the one with the elementary school across the street—a friend called to tell me that Laura was going to be at church that night—and I absolutely had to come meet her finally. It was late, almost time for church, and I had been working on my bike that afternoon and was grimy. But I decided to give it one last shot.

Walking into church, I realized I looked pretty scruffy. I

had my biker boots on and an old biker T-shirt that someone had given me. I figured if she was looking for Mr. Conservative, I wasn't it. But, what the heck, this was the real me.

And then I saw her.

I was stunned. I hadn't seen any pictures of her yet. If there's ever such a thing as love at first sight, it was then. This girl was beautiful.

And then we talked.

And we kept talking.

And we talked some more.

We went on a date, then we went on another.

About a week later we made plans to go surfing together, but when we got to the beach, the water was completely flat. God must have planned that, because our surfboards stayed strapped to the car, and we walked on the beach instead. We talked and talked and talked.

That date was it. I was done. I knew it. I wanted to marry this girl. She was the one.

Two weeks after that, Laura and I found ourselves driving out to Palm Springs to see my parents, who were staying there. I had already talked to Laura's parents, and they gave us their blessing. My parents were a lot less sure. Actually, they thought I was crazy. But I told them, "You've just got to meet her." So my folks met her and they fell in love with her immediately. My dad gave us his blessing and prayed for us. On the drive back from Palm Springs, Laura and I stopped at the Ontario mall and found a twenty-dollar ring in a kiosk. Right there in the middle of the mall, I got down on one knee and proposed.

She said yes.

A couple of weeks later on Valentine's Day, I got her a real ring and proposed again.

She still said yes.

So that June we held our wedding ceremony on the beach. It was early evening, and all our closest friends and family were there. Jim Burns, a minister and great friend of mine, performed the ceremony. Laura looked absolutely amazing. She walked down the aisle to the Beach Boy's "Surfer Girl" and the sound of waves. My ninety-four-year-old grandmother was also there. She can hardly hear at all and talked throughout the entire ceremony. About halfway through she leaned over to my mom and said, really loudly: "Ryan's not wearing shoes."

Everyone smiled. There was no pressure here. It was just an evening for warmth and celebration, and knowing that God ordains our lives in ways we could never dream.

Laura and I spent our honeymoon in Tahiti. A friend set us up in this incredible hotel. It looked like a movie set. We surfed, and lazed around, and talked with the locals. The water was the bluest I've ever seen—the ocean in Tahiti makes Hawaii look like a mud puddle.

Laura is a better surfer than I am. She's absolutely amazing. She'd drop into waves I wouldn't touch. The locals all thought this was pretty funny—here's this five-two, hundred pound blonde girl out on these enormous waves. But we didn't care. **We were together, and our life was starting,** and the future looked bright.

A PLACE TO START

But that's my story. And this book is really about yours. So what's all this "married happily every after" stuff about?

Think about this: A marriage ceremony is a lot like accepting Christ. It's a happy day. An incredible moment in life. But life doesn't stop there. It's really meant to be the place to start.

The best kind of marriage doesn't happen when you stay in your tux, never leave the church, or just stay away forever under a palm tree. A wedding really matters because of what's just beginning—a life together, a shared dream, a bigger idea of what life could be than before you shared your vows and kissed.

Same goes for the abundant life in Christ. Getting saved was really meant to be the happy beginning, the place to start on the adventure of the rest of your life.

I know Laura and I will experience both good and bad moments throughout the rest of our lives. We're prepared for that. Life won't be all about honeymoons in Tahiti. And there are both good and bad moments in the Christian journey, too. But you were born to live for something truly significant, and you can't get there if you're unwilling to leave the security of your now-I'm-saved-and-satisfied wedding chapel...and begin your life's adventure with God.

When you take a good, honest look at your life, are you merely a "social hour" Christian, content that you have an insurance policy against hell?

Or do you long for something more? **Do you long to truly live the abundant life Christ offers?**

That kind of life means a lot will change, a lot more will break loose—but you don't have to do it on your own because you're relying on God.

It means you understand your weaknesses and limitations without letting them defeat you because you know the Holy Spirit is at work in you and through you anyway.

It means people look at you and say in a good way, "Wow! You're different, you know? You're not like everybody else. You've got something better."

Are you ready for that? I hope so.

If you remember only one thing from this book, I would want it to be this: The abundant life I've been talking about is *right here, right now,* and it's found *in one person, Jesus Christ.* When you know Him, and spend time knowing Him, your life is wilder than you could ever imagine. No, your life won't always seem abundant, but God will be at work in you to bring forth life in you and in others.

But that's it. That's the happy beginning. Your life today begins with Christ—and goes from there to more than you can imagine.

Don't settle for anything less.

EXTRA STUFF

Discussion/Reflection Guide

(with Help for Group Leaders)

Thanks for reading my book. I've included some discussion and going-deeper ideas here because I want to help you think and talk through the message of *2 Live 4*. Use this little section either for your personal use or in a group. (If you're a group leader, look at the end for some special help just for you.) Take it chapter by chapter, ask the Holy Spirit to lead you, and look for good things!

Ryan

CHAPTER 1. WHEN YOU RIDE TO HELL'S KITCHEN

The Big Idea

Once you're a Christian, you've got a free ticket to heaven. But that's for later. What about now? You haven't been saved just to be safe (and bored). You've been called to a journey. You've been reborn for a rich, overflowing life that the Bible calls "abundant." This abundant life isn't a formula, isn't pain proof, and won't always come easy. But it's real. It's a daily relationship with Jesus. And it's a life that overflows with the best that our good God has to offer. And by the way, our God is very, very good!

Talk About It

1. Talk about your experience of coming to know Jesus Christ. What did it feel like? At the time, what did you expect the rest of your Christian life to be like?

2. Are you more energized by risk or by security? The journey or the arrival?

3. Ryan talks about the difference between real motorcycle riders and "trailer queens"—people who like the lifestyle and the look a lot more than the adventure of the ride. Which kind of person do you see most in churches you've been in? Or is it fair to even judge?

4. Read the story of Peter walking on water to Jesus (Matthew 14:22–33). Put yourself in Peter's place. Would you say he was an idiot, an extremist, a man who really trusted Jesus, a guy on a dare...or something else? What does this story teach you that could make a difference in your life today?

5. Ryan tells the story of a personal crisis in his life where God seemed far away. How about you—have you ever been through an experience that left you feeling bro-

ken? How did things resolve, if they did? What do you think God might want you to learn today about the Christian life from that experience?

CHAPTER 2. THE STRETCH OF FAITH

The Big Idea

Feeling the presence of God is so wonderful and powerful, but sometimes…well, sometimes we don't feel Him in our lives at all. Does that mean we're not on to the abundant life He promises? No. What we need at times like that is a lot of one little word—faith. Faith means we trust God even when we don't see Him. Faith is what lets God be God, and do amazing things, in situations that seem impossible.

Talk About It

1. Cool morning, quiet water, paddling out on a board in search of the right wave—that's when Ryan really feels God's presence. What about you? Describe your best time and place to meet with God.

2. Have you ever really been at the end of your rope—broke, beat up, and feeling like a loser? Talk about it. Are you still there now, or have you moved on?

3. At the time when you're called to take the stretch of faith, how do you usually feel? Smart or like a loser? Spiritual or full of doubts? Proud or humbled?

4. Hebrews 11:1 reads, "Now faith is being sure of what we hope for and certain of what we do not see." Why is that kind of faith so hard for most people?

5. What could change for the better in your Christian life if you decided to really live by faith?

CHAPTER 3. LOOSENING THE DEATH GRIP

The Big Idea

Entitlement means you think you've got the good life coming to you whether you actually earn it or not. It's wrong and dumb. But that's how many people approach their Christianity too—*I'm saved. You owe me, God. Now pay up.* But to get to the abundant life, we have to get past those lies. We have to start taking risks in God's direction, and leave the results up to Him. Is His plan crazy? Sometimes it sure seems like it. But He's never let anyone down yet.

Talk About It

1. Ryan calls entitlement thinking "poison in your blood." What do you think he means? How can the same kind

of thinking (hanging on to our so-called rights and privileges) poison a follower of Christ?

2. "Slacker spirituality"—ouch, that hurts! Ever felt like your faith deserved that title? Why?

3. Take a minute to think about the attitudes or assumptions you bring with you into your relationship with God or to the church: Do you see any entitlement thinking happening? Any areas where you're holding on to what you think God or the church "owes" you? If so, are you motivated to make changes? Talk about it.

4. Check out a copy of *Under the Overpass*, by Mike Yankoski, or go to undertheoverpass.com. What's your reaction to Mike's choice to live homeless for six months to put his faith to the test and learn what God had to teach him? Would you consider a similar, radical experiment of faith? If so, describe it. Are you willing to pray seriously about your idea?

5. On a long bike ride, Ryan learned to see his parent's life of faithful ministry in a new light. Who are the most inspiring examples of faithfulness and trusting God in your life? What do they do that's so impressive?

CHAPTER 4. THE HARDEST PART

The Big Idea

If you're a high energy, go-over-the-edge-now kind of person, the hardest part of the abundant life might just be the pacing. For example, God doesn't get in a rush very often (maybe never). Often, He asks us to go slow. We end up in long, empty, waterless stretches. We wonder, *Does God care about me, about my dreams?* But when we start thinking like that, look out! Dumb shortcuts can start to look very appealing. At these times, God asks us to believe that no matter what circumstances look like, He's with us, and He loves us, He's at work on something good.

Talk About It

1. Ever found yourself stuck on one of those "strange loops"—waiting, nothing makes sense, nothing seems to get you anywhere, and you're stuck in the middle of nowhere? Talk about it. How did that experience affect your emotions? Your relationships with others, including your relationship with God?

2. Look at the story of Abram and Sarai again (Genesis 12–17). Why do you think it was easier for Abram to believe God when he was first called to leave Ur than it was for him and his wife to wait for years—decades, actually—for God to deliver on His promises?

3. What are some emotions or temptations that you feel most vulnerable to when you feel stuck, forgotten, or abandoned?

4. Ryan writes: "One caution here: To wait does not mean to do nothing." Any thoughts on what he means? On the dangers of not being clear about the difference?

5. Ryan also gives this advice: "I believe it's especially important to get wise counsel from Christians who are older than we are." Why is that advice hard to put into practice for a lot of people these days? Is it for you? If so, ask your friends to help you problem-solve.

CHAPTER 5. IN THE GRIT

The Big Idea

Could the abundant life really be happening when bad things happen? When things break? When we suffer? When we've come to the end of ourselves? Yes! In fact, we might be on the brink of a personal transformation or deliverance. Look at Jehoshaphat and his people in 2 Chronicles 20— things didn't turn around for them until they admitted, "We don't know what to do, but our eyes are on You." That's when God really went to work.

Talk About It

1. Have you ever been broken down beside the road, in the dark, and out of ideas about what to do next? Talk about it. What did you feel? What happened eventually?

2. It's the things that go wrong when we're on a road trip or out recreating that we tend to remember and talk about later with the most feeling. Why do you suppose that is?

3. Why is it so easy for most of us to get angry at God when we're unhappy or suffering in our personal lives? Read Isaiah 26:3–4. What kind of response would be smarter and more pleasing to God?

4. What helps you get your perspective back when things are not going well? Any thoughts, verses, or activities that you could recommend?

5. Ryan writes, "A God-sent adventure is always bigger than us." Do you agree with him? If so, why?

CHAPTER 6. THE PEOPLE THAT DRIVE US NUTS

The Big Idea

We're called to live in and care about the community of believers. But some people seem impossible to deal with— and some people think the same thing about us! How do we get from that kind of discomfort to the abundant life?

First, people are different, and we don't all fit easily together. Second, we need to take responsibility for our own shortcomings (that can be humbling!). And third, working things out with others is an important way God makes us more like His Son, Jesus.

Talk About It

1. So if we're reborn in Christ when we get saved, why are so many Christians so hard to get along with? Do we tend to expect relationships to be different (easier) with Christians than with non-Christians?

2. What kind of "jerk" tends to upset you the most? What might that tell you about yourself?

3. Paul writes in Romans 12:18, "If it is possible, as far as it depends on you, live at peace with all men." How would you say you're doing at following that advice? What relationship conflicts might move toward resolution if you were more proactive for peace?

4. Ryan talks about taking responsibility for the challenges that come from being A.D.D. Are there behaviors or habits in your life where you find it much easier to blame others or make excuses for than to take personal responsibility? Talk about them or write them out. Ask God to show you what change needs to happen.

5. Accountability relationships are like guardrails on a mountain road—you don't seem to need them until you *really* need them! Are you accountable to a person or persons in your life? How is that working for you?

CHAPTER 7. ONE DAY SHE MADE A CHOICE

The Big Idea

Small choices can make the biggest differences imaginable. No wonder God cares about our choices, large and small. Large as in who we marry. Small as in how we treat a waitress. When we blow it, we need His grace, but He wants us to get up, make amends, and begin again. Making the right choices—you could call it obedience to God—takes courage, especially if no one's watching or those who are support the *wrong* choice.

Talk About It

1. Ryan tells the story of tuning out the person in the airplane next to him, even when he knew the guy was open spiritually. Have you ever honestly, consciously, completely shut-down when you *knew* you were being invited by the Holy Spirit to speak up for Christ? Talk about it. How do you feel about that experience now?

2. Identify one small choice that you seem to struggle the most with? Is it a public or a private one? Do you see any progress in that area (assuming you're trying)? What might this little battle tell you about yourself?

3. Is there a huge choice that you're facing that you don't seem to have the courage to make? Can you talk or

write about that? How could the abundant life God promises actually be on the other side of a right decision?

4. Is there a wrong decision or failure of courage in your past that you still struggle with? Take some time to journal about it. Read these Bible passages prayerfully: Psalm 25, Isaiah 43, Luke 15, 1 John 1:5–10. What step of faith in God's goodness do you feel He might be asking you to take?

5. Do you think independent, adventure-oriented people have more trouble obeying God than more security-oriented believers, or less? Or might they just struggle in different areas?

CHAPTER 8. JUST PREACH IT

The Big Idea

Every disciple of Jesus Christ is called to preach the good news in word and deed. Unfortunately, many of us look for excuses to leave it up to the "preacher" who works for our church. The gospel is so simple that anyone can share it and receive it. We can be real. We can be us. But we need to just say it in whatever ways we can. That invites the Holy Spirit to do what only He can do—draw another soul to Christ.

Talk About It

1. Have you thought of yourself as a preacher before? Why or why not?

2. Have you every tried to share the gospel and totally bombed? Talk about it. Do you think God could have been at work anyway?

3. Do you think God can work through you, sharing the gospel even when there are things in your life that are messed up? Why?

4. Often people with little speaking ability or "stage presence" are the ones people listen to and believe first. Why do you think that's so?

5. Could you identify one or more people in your life that you've sensed might be "appointments" waiting for you to speak up about Jesus Christ? Are you willing to pray about making a decision to act?

CHAPTER 9. OPEN THROTTLE HERE

The Big Idea

You weren't saved for a happy ending—at least not here on earth. You were saved for something better—a strong start down a very important life journey. But opening the throttle is up to you. You can do "everything" through Him who gives you strength (Philippians 4:13). And along the way, our amazingly good God will surprise you with a lot more joy and a much better life than you could ever pull off on your own. Travel plan for every day from here on: *Stay close to the person and heart of Jesus Christ. The rest is details.*

Talk About It

1. In what ways was becoming a Christian an ending for you? In what ways was it a beginning?

2. Are you ready to "get on and open the throttle" of your life with Christ? Talk about it. What would you like to change, starting right away?

3. Ryan tells about how—against all odds—the Lord brought Laura into his life. Do you have a story of God's surprising goodness in your life? If so, talk about it.

4. Why might it be important for you to remember your own "God is surprisingly good" stories and talk about them often?

5. Picture your life three years from now. How would you like the abundant life of Christ to be evident in you by then? That picture could be your *2 Live 4* life! Right down what you hope for and say it to God often in the weeks and months ahead.

HELP FOR GROUP LEADERS

You can have a blast guiding a discussion group through
this book. While you're helping them get in touch with
God's plans for an adventure-filled life, you'll learn a lot
about yourself too.

Some quick reminders:

—Encourage everyone to individually read through all of
   2 Live 4. Stay open to whatever questions the group
   members have as a result of interacting with the content.

—Lots of questions will probably come up. Lots of different opinions might be expressed. Whenever possible, go
   to the Scriptures together to look for God's answers and
   perspectives. Use the Scriptures to help keep God in
   charge of your discussion. Encourage everyone in your
   group to hear His voice coming through in the pages of
   the Bible.

—Set an example by responding honestly to the teaching
   in this book. All of us have a lot of room to grow in
   learning how to live out this book's message. So be can-
   did about your personal needs. As you face them
   honestly, you'll be encouraging others in the group to
   do the same.

—Discuss together how you can support and encourage
   one another in this commitment to reaching for the
   abundant life Jesus promises.

—Pray for your group members. Pray together with them, and pray for each of them on your own. Ask God to be at work, and thank Him ahead of time (by faith) for what He will do. Ask His Holy Spirit to be the group's teacher.

—As you pray, ask God to protect this group from disunity, selfishness, and pride. Ask for the Holy Spirit to give all of you spiritual insight into His truths from the Bible. Ask for the personal discoveries and breakthroughs that are most needed in each person's life.

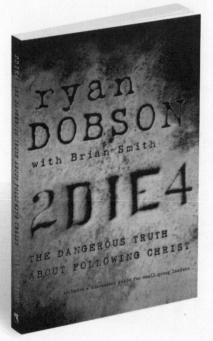

BE INTOLERANT

Our Generation Is Being Destroyed by Rampant Tolerance

Alarming numbers of Christians eighteen to twenty-five years old don't believe in absolute truth. Impassioned youth speaker Ryan Dobson exposes the world's famine for absolute truth—and shows how to fight it.

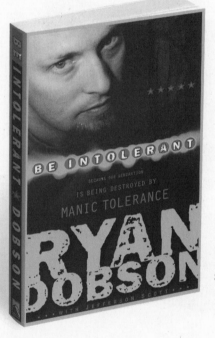

1-59052-152-8
$10.99

Under the Overpass

Two guys. Homeless.
Experiencing God's greatness.
How big is your God?

Mike and Sam found their beds under bridges and received
handouts from strangers for five months...by their own
choice. Mike's firsthand account of how five months on the
streets changed his life may also change yours.

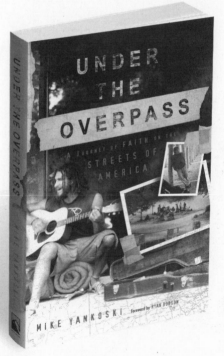